Bethany House Publishers

The Novels of George MacDonald Edited for Today's Reader

MacDonald Classics Edited for Young Readers

Wee Sir Gibbie of the Highlands
Alec Forbes and His Friend Annie
At the Back of the North Wind

George MacDonald: Scotland's Beloved Storyteller
by Michael Phillips
Discovering the Character of God by George MacDonald
Knowing the Heart of God by George MacDonald

GEORGE MACDONALD CLASSIC DEVOTIONALS

A TIME TO HARVEST

Inspiring Devotional Selections from the Writings of

George MacDonald

Compiled and Edited by
Michael R. Phillips

BETHANY HOUSE PUBLISHERS
Minneapolis, Minnesota 55438

ISBN 1-55661-207-9

Published by Bethany House Publishers
A Ministry of Bethany Fellowship, Inc.
6820 Auto Club Road, Minneapolis, Minnesota 55438

Printed in the United States of America

CONTENTS

INTRODUCTION

Scottish novelist and poet George MacDonald (1824–1905) was a writer of such depth and diversity that his books often seem daunting at first glance. If his complex thoughts and lofty spiritual ideas are not enough to overwhelm some, the Scottish dialect in many of his novels can intimidate the most adventurous of readers. Add to this the fact that most of MacDonald's books are over 400 pages in length—sometimes even five, six, or seven hundred in their original editions—and it is not difficult to understand why his readership in the past has been loyal but rather small.

I am one of those few loyal readers, and years ago was born in my heart the vision of reintroducing Mac-Donald to today's readers. I was pleased to find a publisher who shared this vision, and Bethany House Publishers and I teamed up to select, edit, and publish eighteen of his novels to date. The number of books sold since the first one, *The Fisherman's Lady*, was published in 1982 has been gratifying, and even more so are the personal responses from new MacDonald fans.

For years my good friends at Bethany have talked about MacDonald devotional books comprised of brief passages from some of his novels. Our hope is to offer concise selections that capture some of the incidents, relationships, conversations, and observations from MacDonald's stories that highlight his insights and perspectives. For readers familiar with his books, such passages in a devotional format can serve as rewarding reminders of past reading experiences as well as become vehicles for personal encounters with God. For those still unfamiliar with MacDonald, these devotional excerpts offer an introductory exposure to George Mac-

Donald's deep spiritual insight through the characters and events in his novels. Appropriate poetry pieces and parallel selections from his sermons add further insight into MacDonald's breadth of spiritual understanding.

We have built this series of devotional compilations on a seasonal theme, since the yearly changes of nature played such a prominent role in MacDonald's own life and in his stories. *A Time to Harvest* centers on an autumn theme, both literally and figuratively. The publisher and I invite you to let these devotional readings make a time for spiritual harvest in your own life.

Mike Phillips
September, 1991

THE WARMTH OF A FALL FIRE

WITH THE LIBRARY OF LOSSIE HOUSE AT HIS disposal, and almost nothing to do, it might now have been a grand time for Malcolm's studies; but alas! he too often found it all but impossible to keep his thoughts on the track through a single sentence of any length.

The autumn now hung over the verge of its grave. Hoarfrost lay thick on the fields. Summer was indeed gone, and winter was nigh with its storms and its fogs and its rotting rains and its drifting snows. Malcolm sorely missed the ministrations of compulsion: he lacked labor, the most helpful and most healing of all God's holy things.

The Fisherman's Lady, p. 195

For thou shalt eat the labour of thine hands:
happy shalt thou be, and it shall be well
with thee.
Psalm 128:2

To the foundation of yesterday's work well done, the work of tomorrow will be sure to fit. Work *done* is of more consequence for the future than all the foresight and planning of an archangel.

Knowing the Heart of God, p. 72;
Unspoken Sermons, Second Series—"The Cause of Spiritual Stupidity"

GOOD DOCTRINE IS
BAD FOR BUSINESS

"I'LL TAKE ANY OFFER WITHIN REASON FOR HER," said the factor. "You'll just ride her to Forres market next week and see what you can get for her. I do think she's quieter, though, since you took her in hand."

"I'm sure she is, but it won't last a day if she's sold. The moment I leave her she'll be just as bad as ever. She has a kind of liking to me because I give her sugar and she can't throw me, but she's no better in her heart yet. She's an unsanctified brute. I couldn't think of selling her like this."

"Let whoever buys beware," said the factor.

"Oh, yes, let them! I don't object as long as they know what she's like before they buy her," rejoined Malcolm.

The factor burst out laughing. To his judgment, the youth had spoken like an idiot. "We'll not send you to sell," he said. "Stoat shall go with you, and you shall have nothing to do but hold the mare and your own tongue."

"Sir," said Malcolm seriously, "you don't mean what you say? You said yourself she'd be the death of somebody, and to sell her without telling what she's like would be to break the sixth commandment clean to shivers."

"That may be good doctrine in church, my lad, but it's pure heresy in the horse market. No, no! You buy a horse as you take a wife—for better or worse, as the case may be. A woman's not bound to tell her faults when a man wants to marry her."

"Hoot, sir! There's no comparison. Mistress Kelpie here's plenty ready to confess her faults by giving anyone who wants to know a taste of them—she won't even wait

to be asked. And if you expect me to hold my tongue about them, Mr. Crathie, I'd as soon think of selling Blue Peter a rotten boat. And, besides, there's the eighth commandment as well as the sixth. There's no exceptions about horseflesh. We must be as honest with that as anything else."

The Marquis' Secret, p. 8

Bread of deceit is sweet to a man;
but afterwards his mouth shall be
filled with gravel.
Proverbs 20:17

The one cure for any being is to be set right—to have all its parts brought into harmony with each other. The one comfort is to know that this cure is in process. Rightness alone is cure. To free a man or woman from suffering, he or she must be set right, put in health. And the health at the root of man's being, his rightness, is to be free from wrongness that is, from sin. The wrong, the evil is *in* him. He must be set free from it. To do this for us, Jesus was born, and remains born to all the ages.

Knowing the Heart of God, p. 213;
The Hope of the Gospel—"Salvation From Sin"

13

THE DELIGHT OF CREATION IS IN SECRETS

AS DONAL WALKED, THE SCENTS THE WIND brought him from the field and gardens and moor seemed sweeter than before, for they were seeking to comfort him. The wind hovered about him as if it would fain have something to do in the matter; the river rippled and shone as if it knew something worth knowing as yet unrevealed. The delight of creation is verily in secrets, but in secrets as truths on the way. And as he made his way, already something of the old mysterious loveliness—which had temporarily vanished from his awareness—of the face of the visible world had returned to it, with the dawning promise of a new creation, ready to receive the new that God had waiting for him. He would look the new life in the face and be what it should please God to make him. *The Shepherd's Castle, p. 12*

And the Lord shall guide thee continually,
and satisfy thy soul in drought, and make fat
thy bones: and thou shalt be like a watered
garden, and like a spring of water, whose
waters fail not.
Isaiah 58:11

THE END OF THE HOLIDAY

THE MORNING AT LENGTH ARRIVED WHEN Robert and Shargar must return to Rothieden. A keen autumnal wind was blowing far-off feathery clouds across a sky of pale blue. The cold freshened the spirits of the boys and tightened their nerves and muscles till they were like bow strings. No doubt the winter was coming, but the sun, although his day's work was short and slack, was still as clear as ever. So gladsome was the world that the boys received the day as a fresh holiday, and strenuously forgot tomorrow.

After they had said farewell—in which Shargar seemed to suffer more than Robert—and had turned the corner of the stables, they heard the good farmer shouting after them. "They'll be another harvest next year, boys," which wonderfully restored their spirits.

The Musician's Quest, p. 109

While the earth remaineth, seedtime and harvest, and cold and heat, and summer and winter, and day and night shall not cease.
Genesis 8:22

The whole secret of progress is doing the thing we know. There is no other way of progress in the spiritual life, no other way of progress in the understanding of that life. Only as we do, can we know. *Knowing the Heart of God, p. 43;*
Unspoken Sermons, Second Series—"The Truth in Jesus"

When the Scriptures Become Real

IT WAS A VERY HUMBLE DWELLING, BUILT OF turf upon a foundation of stones, and roofed with turf and straw—warm, and nearly impervious to the searching airs of the mountainside. One little window of a foot and half square looked out on the universe. At one end stood a stack of peat, half as big as the cottage itself. All around it were huge rocks. A few of the commonest flowers grew about the door, but there was no garden. The doorstep was natural stone, and a huge projecting rock behind formed the back and a portion of one of the end walls. This latter rock had been the attraction to the site because of a hollow in it, which now served as a dairy. For up there with them lived the last cow of the valley— the cow that breathed the loftiest air on all Daurside, a good cow, gifted in feeding well upon little.

Gibbie knocked at the old, weather-beaten, well-patched door. "Come on in, whoever ye be."

Gibbie pulled the string that came through a hole in the door; so lifting the latch, he entered.

A woman sat on a stool, her face turned over her shoulder to see who came. It was a grey face, with good, simple features and clear eyes. The plentiful hair that grew low on her forehead was half grey, mostly covered by a white cap with frills. A clean apron of blue print over a blue petticoat completed her dress. A book lay on her lap. Always when she had finished her morning's work and made her house tidy, she sat down to have her "comfort," as she called it. The moment she saw Gibbie

she rose. She was rather a little woman and carried herself straight and light.

"Eh, ye poor outcast!" she said in the pitying voice of a mother. "How did ye get up here? And what do you want here? I have nothing."

Receiving no answer but one of the child's bewitching smiles, she stood for a moment regarding him, not in mere silence but with a look of dumbness. She was a mother and, more, one of God's mothers.

Now the very moment before Gibbie entered, she had been reading the words of the Lord: "Inasmuch as ye have done it unto one of the least of these, ye have done it unto me"; and with her heart full of them, she had lifted her eyes and seen Gibbie. For one moment, with the quick flashing response of the childlike imagination of the Celt, she fancied she saw the Lord himself.

The Baronet's Song, pp. 42–43

Be not forgetful to entertain strangers: for thereby some have entertained angels unawares.
Hebrews 13:2

A man must not choose his neighbor. He must take the neighbor that God sends him. In him, whoever he or she be, lies either hidden or revealed a beautiful brother or sister. The neighbor is just the man or woman or child who is next to you at this very moment, he or she with whom *any* business, even any seeming accident of life, has brought you in contact.
Knowing the Heart of God, p. 331;
Unspoken Sermons, First Series—"Love Thy Neighbor"

ALL THINGS WILL BE SET RIGHT IN THE END

WITHOUT THESE TWO MAIN PILLARS OF life, necessity and duty, how shall the temple stand, when the huge, weary Samson comes tugging at it? The wonder is that there is not a great deal more wickedness in the world. For listlessness and boredness and nothing-to-do-ness are the best of soils for the breeding of the worms that never stop gnawing; and parents especially who would keep their children from becoming the future Toms and Sepias of the world would do well to provide them with plenty of materials to make the pillars of their temples strong, in the form of necessities and duties.

Anyhow, Sepia had flashed on Tom. The tinder of Tom's heart had responded, and any day when Sepia chose, she might blow up a wicked as well as a foolish flame. And if it should suit her purpose, Sepia was not one to hesitate in the use of the fire-fan. All the way home her eyes haunted him, and it is a more dreadful thing than most are aware of to be haunted by anything, good or bad, except the being who is out of life. And those eyes, though not good, were beautiful. Evil, it is true, has neither part nor lot in beauty; it is absolutely hostile to it, and will at last destroy it utterly. But the process is a long one, so long that many imagine badness and beauty vitally associable. Tom yielded to the haunting, and it was in part the fault of those eyes that he used such hard words on his wife in the morning. Wives often suffer sorely for discomforts and wrongs in their husbands of which they know nothing. But the thing will be set right one day, and in a better fashion than if all

18

the women's-rights committees in the world had their will of the matter. *A Daughter's Devotion, p. 183*

Let us hear the conclusion of the whole matter:
Fear God, and keep his commandments: for
this is the whole duty of man.
Ecclesiastes 12:13

The cause of every man's discomfort is evil, moral evil. First of all evil in himself, his own sin, his own wrongness, his own unrightness. Then secondly, evil in those he loves. With this latter, the only way to get rid of it is for the man to get rid of his *own* sin.

Foolish is the man, and there are many such men, who would rid himself or his fellows of discomfort by setting the world right, by waging war on the evils around him, while he neglects that integral part of the world where lies his business, his first business—namely, his own character and conduct. Even if it were possible—an absurd supposition—that the world should thus be righted from the outside, it would still be impossible for such a man, remaining what he was, to enjoy the perfection of the result, for he would yet be out of tune with the organ he had tuned.

No evil can be cured in mankind except by its being cured in individual men and women. Rightness alone is cure. *Discovering the Character of God, p. 37;*
The Hope of the Gospel—"Salvation From Sin"

HARVESTING THE EARTH'S LIFE

HUGH HAD WATCHED THE GREEN GRAIN grow, and ear, and turn dim; then brighten to yellow, and ripen at last under the declining autumn sun. The long threads, on each of which hung an oat grain, had become dry and brittle, and the grains began to spread out their chaff-wings as if ready to fly. They rustled with sweet sounds against each other as the wind swept gently and tenderly over the fields. The harvest here was mostly of oats, and they hung most gracefully of all; next bowed the bearded barley; and stately and strong stood the fields of wheat, of a rich, ruddy, golden hue. Above the yellow harvest rose the purple hills, and above the hills the pale blue autumnal sky.

At length the day arrived to put the sickle to the barley, to be followed by the scythe in the oats. And then came the joy of labor. *The Tutor's First Love, p. 27*

For the Lord thy God bringeth thee into a good land, a land of brooks of water, of fountains and depths that spring out of valleys and hills; a land of wheat, and barley, and vines, and fig trees, and pomegranates; a land of oil olive, and honey.
Deuteronomy 8:7—8

CAN IT BE GOD?

A COLD HAND GRASPING HER HEART, IAN'S mother rose and went from the room. What she had only feared in her son, she knew now! It broke her heart and she lay down as one sick. Such was the hold the authority of traditional human dogma had on her soul. Instead of glorifying God that she had given birth to such a God-loving, free-thinking man, she wept bitterly because he was on the broad road to eternal condemnation.

But even as she lay weeping, something quiet stole over her. Suddenly there rose up in her a moonlight of peace. "Can it be God?" she said to herself.

She could tell no more than Ian whether it was God or not. But from that moment on she began to lift up her heart in such prayer as she had never prayed before. And slowly, imperceptibly the feeling awoke in her that if she was not believing in God as she should, he would help her to believe as she ought to believe. Therewith she began to feel as if the gulf between her and her son were not so wide as she had thought. Doubtless he was in rebellion against God, seeing he would question God's ways, but surely something might yet be done for him! She little suspected the glory of sky and earth and sea eternal that would one day burst upon her, that she would one day see God not only good but infinitely good—infinitely better than she had dared to think him!

The Highlander's Last Song, p. 87

The goodness of God
leadeth thee to repentance.
Romans 2:4

A TIME TO HARVEST

SUMMER FLOWED INTO AUTUMN AND THERE was no sign of the coming vengeance of heaven. The green grain turned pale at last before the gaze of the sun. The life within had done its best and now shrank back to the earth. Anxious farmers watched their fields and joyfully noted every shade of progress. All day the sun shone strong, and all night the moon leaned down from heaven to see how things were going and to keep the work gently moving. At length the new revelation of ancient life was complete, and the grain stood in living gold, and men began to put it to the sickle because the time of harvest was come.

But the feelings with which the master longed for the harvest holiday were sadly different from those of his boys. It was a delight to his students to think of having nothing to do on those glorious hot days but to gather blueberries or lie on the grass or swim in the Glamour and dry themselves in the sun ten times a day. For the master, he only hoped to get away from the six thousand eyes of Glamerton. Not one allusion had been made in his hearing to his dismal degradation, but he knew that was only because it was too dreadful to be alluded to. The tone of additional kindness and consideration with which many addressed him only made him think of what lay behind, and refuse every invitation given him. If he could only get away from everyone's sight, his oppressed heart would begin to revive and he might gather strength to calmly face the continuous pressure in the performance of his duty to the boys and girls of Glamerton.

At length the slow hour arrived. Longing thoughts had almost obliterated the figures upon Time's dial and made it look a hopeless, undivided circle of eternity. But at length twelve o'clock on Saturday came; and the

delight would have been almost unendurable to some had it not been calmed by the dreary closeness of the Sabbath lying between them and freedom. Almost the moment the *amen* of the final prayer was out of the master's mouth, the first boys were shouting jubilantly in the open air. Truffey, who was always the last, was crutching it out after the rest when he heard the master's voice calling him back. He obeyed it with misgiving, so much had fear become a habit.

"Ask your grandfather, Andrew, if he will allow you to go down to the seaside with me for two or three weeks," said the master.

"Yes, sir," Truffey meant to say, but the attempt produced instead an unearthly screech of delight, with which he went off in a series of bounds worthy of a kangaroo, lasting all the way to his grandfather's and taking him there in half the usual time.

And the master and Truffey did go down to the sea together. The master borrowed a gig and hired a horse and driver. They all three sat in the space meant for two. To Truffey a lame leg or two was hardly to be compared with the exultant glory of that day. Was he not the master's friend from now on? And was he not riding with him in a gig—bliss supreme? Truffey was prouder than Mr. Malison could have been if he had been judged to surpass Mr. Turnbull himself in every pulpit gift. And if there be joy in the universe, what is the difference how it be divided?—whether the master be raised from the desk to the pulpit, or Truffey have a ride in a gig?

The Maiden's Bequest, pp. 186–187

To every thing there is a season, and a time to
every purpose under the heaven.
Ecclesiastes 3:1

I WANTED GOD TO LOVE EVERYBODY

THE AMBITION TO MINISTER TO HER FELLOW beings had long lain dormant in Hester's heart. The sight of the poor man in the hall had suddenly awakened something within her and she would never be the same again. She found the feeling growing inside that the whole human family was depending upon her, and that she could not rise in life—even with all the advantages her favored station seemed to offer—without desiring to raise them along with her. For the necessities of our deepest nature do not allow us contentment in mere personal satisfaction. We were not made to live alone. I well remember feeling as a child that I did not want God to love me if he did not love everybody. I had been taught that God chooses some but not others. My very being recoiled from the hint of such a false idea. Even were I one of the few, the chosen, the elect, I could not accept love from such a God. The kind of love I needed was essential to my nature—the same love that *all* men needed, the love that belonged to them as the children of the Father, a love he could not give me unless he gave it to all men.   *The Gentlewoman's Choice, p. 24*

*And to know the love of Christ, which
passeth knowledge, that ye might be filled
with all the fulness of God.*
Ephesians 3:19

LEARN TO JUDGE FOR YOURSELF

AS THEY WALKED, COSMO'S FATHER TOLD him he had been thinking all night what the best thing would be to do with him, and that he had come to the conclusion to ask his friend Peter Simon—the wits of the neighborhood called him Simon Peter—to take charge of his education.

"He is a man of peculiar opinions," he said, "as I daresay you may have heard. But everything in him is on a scale so grand that to fear harm from him would be to sin against the truth. A man must learn to judge for himself, and he will teach you that. I have seen in him so much that I recognize as good and great that I am compelled to believe in him, even where the things he believes appear to me to be out of line, or even extravagant. A man's character must sometimes go a long way to cause you to believe in him, even where in matters of mere opinion—not nearly so important a thing as character—you find that you differ."

The Laird's Inheritance, p. 59

*Because thou . . . hast not asked for thyself
long life; neither hast asked riches for thyself,
nor hast asked the life of thine enemies; but
hast asked for thyself understanding to
discern judgment; Behold, I have done
according to thy words: lo, I have given thee
a wise and an understanding heart; so that
there was none like thee before thee, neither
after thee shall any arise like unto thee.*

1 Kings 3:11–12

WAKING UP OUT OF PROFESSIONAL CHURCH SERVICE

THE WEEKS PASSED AND SEEMED TO BRING him no light, but only increased the earnestness of his search after it. He would have to find an answer before long, he thought, or he would have no choice but to resign his curacy and look for a position as a tutor.

Of course all this he ought to have gone through long ago. But how can a man go through anything till his hour is come? Wingfold had all this time been skirting the wall of the kingdom of heaven without even knowing there was a wall there, not to say seeing a gate in it. The fault lay with those who had introduced him to the church as a profession, just as they might introduce someone to the practice of medicine, or the bar, or the drapery business—as if the ministry were on the same level of choice with other human callings. Never had he been warned to take off his shoes for the holiness of the ground. And yet how were they to have warned him when they themselves had never discovered the treasure in that ground more holy than libraries, incomes, and the visits of royalty? As to visions of truth that make a man sigh with joy and enlarge his heart with more than human tenderness—how many of those men had ever found such treasures in the fields of the church? How many of them knew, except by hearsay, whether there be any Holy Ghost? How then could they warn other men from the dangers of following in their footsteps and becoming such as they? Where in a community of general ignorance shall we begin to blame? Wingfold had

no time to accuse anyone. He simply had to awaken from the dead and cry for light, and was soon in the bitter agony of the paralyzing struggle between life and death.

He thought afterward, when the time had passed, that surely in this period of darkness he had been upheld by a power whose presence he was completely unaware of. He did not know how else he could have gotten through it. Strange helps came to him from time to time. The details of nature wonderfully softened toward him, and for the first time he began to notice her ways and shows and to see in them all the working of an infinite humanity. He later remembered how a hawthorn bud once set him weeping; and how once, as he was walking miserably to church, a child looked up in his face and smiled. In the strength of that smile, he had been able to confidently approach the lectern.

He never knew how long he had been in the agony of his most peculiar birth—in which the soul is at the same time both the mother that bears and the child that is born.   *The Curate's Awakening, p. 39*

I call heaven and earth to record this day
against you, that I have set before you life
and death, blessing and cursing: therefore
choose life, that both thou and
thy seed may live.
Deuteronomy 30:19

WAKE, THOU THAT SLEEPEST, AND COME OUT OF THY GRAVE

"IF A MAN HOLDS ON PRACTICIN' WHAT HE does ken, the hunger'll wake in him after more. I'm thinkin' the angels desired long afore they could see into certain things they wanted t' ken aboot. But ye may be sure they werena left withoot as much light as would lead honest fowk safely on."

"But suppose they couldn't tell whether what they thought they saw was true light or not?"

"Then they would have to fall back upon the will o' the great Light. We ken well enough that he wants us all t' see as he himsel' sees. If we seek that Light, we'll reach it; if we carena for it, we're gaein' nowhere, an' may come in sore need o' some sharp discipline."

"I'm afraid I can't quite follow you. The fact is, I have been so long occupied with the Bible history, and the new discoveries that bear upon it, that I have had but little time for such spiritual metaphysics."

"An' what is the good o' history, or such metaphysics as ye call it as is the very soul o' history, but to help ye see Christ? An' what's the good o' Christ but sae to see God wi' yer heart an' yer understandin' both as t' ken that ye're seein' him, an' sae to receive him into yer very nature? Ye mind hoo the Lord said that none could ken his Father but him to whom the Son would reveal him? Sir, 'tis time ye had a glimpse o' that! Ye ken naethin' till ye ken God—an' he's the only person a man truly can ken in his heart."

"Well, you must be a long way ahead of me, and for the present I'm afraid there's nothing for it but to say good-night to you."

And with the words the minister departed.

"Lord," said the soutar, as he sat guiding his awl through the sole and welt of the shoe he was working on, "there's surely somethin' at work in the yoong man! Surely he canna be that far from wakin' up to see and ken that he sees and kens nothin'. Lord, put down the dyke o' learnin' an' self-righteousness that he canna see over the top o', an' let him see thee on the other side o' it. Lord, send him the grace o' open eyes, to see where an' what he is, that he may cry oot wi' the rest o' us, poor blind bodies, to them that won't see, 'Wake, thou that sleepest, an' come oot o' thy grave, an see the light o' thy grave, an' see the light o' the Father in the face o' the Son.'"

The Minister's Restoration, pp. 63–64

For the Jews require a sign, and the Greeks
seek after wisdom: But we preach Christ
crucified, unto the Jews a stumblingblock,
and unto the Greeks foolishness; but unto
them which are called, both Jews and Greeks,
Christ the power of God, and the
wisdom of God.
1 Corinthians 1:22–24

Demands unknown before are continually being made upon the Christian. It is the ever-fresh rousing and calling, asking and sending of the Spirit that works in the children of obedience.

Knowing the Heart of God, p. 62;
Unspoken Sermons, Second Series—"The Hardness of the Way"

PROGRESS COMES FROM OBEDIENCE

THE MAINSTAY OF MARY'S SPIRITUAL LIFE WAS her father. From books and sermons she had gotten little good, for in neither had the best come near her. She did very nearly her best to obey, but she was yet, in relation to the gospel, much as the Jews were in relation to their law. They had not yet learned the gospel of their law, and she was yet only serving the law of the gospel. But she was making progress, in simple and pure virtue of her obedience. Show me the person ready to step from any, let it be the narrowest sect of Christian Pharisees into a freer and holier air, and I shall look to find in that person one who, in the midst of the darkness and selfish worldliness—mistaken for holiness—around them, has long been living a life more obedient than the rest.

A Daughter's Devotion, p. 46

I speak after the manner of men because of the infirmity of your flesh: for as ye have yielded your members servants to uncleanness and to iniquity unto iniquity; even so now yield your members servants to righteousness unto holiness. . . . But now being made free from sin, and become servants to God, ye have your fruit unto holiness, and the end everlasting life.
Romans 6:19, 22

WHO CAN TELL HOW THE WAKING COMES?

MRS. GORDON BEGAN GRADUALLY TO realize that the only thing that was then helping her was the strong hand of her son upon her. But there was another help that is never lacking where it can find an entrance; and now for the first time she began tentatively to pray, "Lead me not into temptation."

Undoubtedly, during all the period of her excesses, the soul of the woman in her better moments had been ashamed to know her for the thing she was. And when the sleeping woman God made wakes up to see in what a house she lives, she will soon grasp broom and bucket, and not cease her cleansing while there is so much as a spot left on wall or ceiling or floor.

How the waking comes, who can tell? God knows what he wants us to do, and what we can do, and how to help us. What I have to tell is that the next morning, Mrs. Gordon came down to breakfast, and finding her son already seated at the table, came up behind him, without a word set the bottle with the last glass of whiskey in it before him, went to her place at the table, gave him one sorrowful look, and sat down.

His heart understood and rejoiced.

The Peasant Girl's Dream, pp. 206–207

*And lead us not into temptation, but deliver
us from evil: For thine is the kingdom, and the
power, and the glory, for ever. Amen.*
Matthew 6:13

THE ATHEIST WHO OBEYS VERSUS THE CHRISTIAN WHO DOES NOT

FABER WAS BOTH LOVED AND HONORED BY all whom he had attended. He was in the world's eyes a *good* man. With his fine tastes, his genial nature, his quiet conscience, his good health, his enjoyment of life, his knowledge and love of his profession, his activity, his tender heart—especially to women and children—and his keen intellect, if any man could get on without a God, Faber was that man. He was now trying it, and as yet the trial had cost him no great effort. He seemed to himself to be doing very well indeed.

And why should he not do as well as the thousands who counted themselves "religious" people and who got through the business of the hour, the day, the week, the year without once referring to the will of God or the words of Christ in anything they did or did not do? If he was more helpful to his fellows than they, he fared better as well. For actions which are in themselves good, however imperfect the motives, react wonderfully upon character and nature. It is better to be an atheist who does the will of God than a so-called Christian who does not. The atheist will not be dismissed because he said *Lord, Lord* and did not obey. What God loves is only the lovely thing, and he who does such a thing does well and is on the way to discovering that he does it very badly. When one begins to do the will of the perfect God, then that person is on the road to doing it perfectly.

Doing things from duty is but a stage on the road to the kingdom of truth and love. But because it is but a stage, not the less must that stage be journeyed; every path diverging from that road is "the flowery way that leads to the broad gate and the great fire."

The Lady's Confession, pp. 29–30

Enter ye in at the strait gate: for wide is the gate, and broad is the way, that leadeth to destruction, and many there be which go in thereat.
Matthew 7:13

If those who set themselves to explain the various theories of Christianity had set themselves instead to do the will of the Master, the one object for which the gospel was preached, how different would the world now be! Had they given themselves to understanding his Word that they might do it, and not to buttress their systems of dogma, in many a heart by this time would the name of the Lord be loved where it now remains unknown.

Unhindered by Christians' explanations of Christianity, undeterred by having their acceptance forced on them, but attracted instead by their behavior, men would be saying to each other, as Moses said to himself when he saw the bush that burned but was not consumed, "I will now turn aside and see this great sight!" All over the world, people would be drawing near to behold how these Christians loved one another.

Knowing the Heart of God, pp. 43–44;
Unspoken Sermons, Second Series—"The Truth in Jesus"

TRUE BELIEF IS LIFE

SHE LONGED FOR SOMETHING POSITIVE to believe, something in accordance with which her feelings might agree. She was still on the outlook for definite intellectual formulae to hold. Like so many seeming Christians, she could not divorce her mind from thinking of belief as a framework of viewpoints—social, political, philosophical, and theoretical, none of which the Lord had anywhere in mind when he said, "Repent and *believe* in the gospel." True belief consists in no cognitive convictions, no matter how pious, no matter how biblically correct, but rather in *life* as it is *lived*.

Alexa's interaction with Andrew had as yet failed to open her eyes to the fact that the faith required of us is faith in a person, not in the truest of statements concerning anything, even concerning him, for some do not discern his truth correctly. Neither was she yet alive to the fact that faith in the living One, the very essence of it, consists in obedience to him. A man can obey before he is intellectually sure; and except he obey the command he knows to be right, wherever it may come from, he will never be sure. To find the truth, a man or woman must be true. *The Landlady's Master, p. 173*

*For this cause also thank we God without
ceasing, because, when ye received the word of
God which ye heard of us, ye received it not
as the word of men, but as it is in truth, the
word of God, which effectually worketh also
in you that believe.*
1 Thessalonians 2:13

IF ANY MAN IS WILLING

THE NEXT MORNING JAMES WAS IN THE field with the rest long before the sun was up. Day by day he grew stronger in mind and in body.

His deliverance from the slavery of Sunday prayers and sermons, and his consequent sense of freedom and its delight, greatly favored his growth in health and strength. Before the winter came, however, he had begun to find his heart turning toward the pulpit with a waking desire to again expound God's truths, this time with reality.

One day, with a sudden questioning hunger, he rose in haste from his knees and turned almost trembling to his Greek New Testament, to find whether the words of the Master, "If any man will do the will of the Father," meant "If any man is willing to do the will of the Father." Finding that to be just exactly what they did mean, he was able to be at rest sufficiently to go on asking and hoping. And it was not long thereafter that he began to feel he had something worth telling, and must tell it to anyone that would hear. Heartily he set himself to pray for that spirit of truth, which the Lord had promised to them that asked it of their Father in heaven.

The Minister's Restoration, p. 197

Howbeit when he, the Spirit of truth, is come, he will guide you into all truth: for he shall not speak of himself; but whatsoever he shall hear, that shall he speak: and he will shew you things to come.
John 16:13

INVISIBLE LINES

"SURELY YOU SPEAK YOUR OWN OPINIONS in describing the man."

"I do. He is accountable for nothing I say."

"How is it that so many good people consider him unorthodox and his ways suspect?"

"I do not mind that. To such well-meaning people with small natures, theology must be like a map—with plenty of lines in it. They cannot trust their house on the high tableland of this man's theology because they cannot see the outlines bounding his land. It is not small enough for them. They cannot take it in. Such people, one would think, can hardly be satisfied with creation, seeing there is no line of division anywhere in it."

"Does God draw no lines, then?"

"When he does, they are pure lines, without breadth, and consequently invisible to mortal eyes, not walls of separation such as these definers would construct."

"But is it reasonable that a theory in religion be correct if it is so hard to see?"

"They are only hard to see for certain natures."

"But those people, those natures you speak of, are above average usually. And you have granted them good intentions."

"Generally good, but very narrow perspective."

"Is it not rather hard of you then to say that they cannot understand, cannot perceive truth in the high tableland?"

"Is it hard of me? Why? They will get to heaven, which is all they want. And they will understand one day, which is more than they pray for."

"But who is to say that you are right and they are the unenlightened ones? They could bring the same charge against you, of being unable to understand them."

"Yes. And so it must remain until the Spirit of God decides the matter, which I presume must take place by slow degrees. For this decision can only consist in the enlightenment of souls to see the truth. Till then, the Right must be content to be called the Wrong and—which is far harder—to seem the Wrong. There is no spiritual victory gained by a verbal conquest."

The Tutor's First Love, p. 193

A servant will not he corrected by words: for
though he understand he will not answer.
Proverbs 29:19

When we understand the outside of things, we think we have them. Yet the Lord puts his things in subdefined, suggestive shapes, yielding no satisfactory meaning to the mere intellect, but unfolding themselves to the conscience and heart, to the man himself, in the process of life-effort.

Accordingly, as the new creation, in reality, advances in him, the man becomes able to understand the words, the symbols, the parables of the Lord.

For life, that is, action, is alone the human condition into which the light of the Living can penetrate. Life alone can assimilate life, can change food into growth. *Knowing the Heart of God, pp. 69–70,*

Unspoken Sermons, Second Series—"The Cause of Spiritual Stupidity"

THE ONE THING GOD DESIRES

"Do you really suppose God cares whether a man comes to good or ill?"

"If he did not, he could not be good himself."

"Then you don't think a good God would want to punish poor wretches like us?"

"Your lordship has not been in the habit of regarding himself as a poor wretch. And remember, you can't call a child a poor wretch without insulting the father of it."

"That's quite another thing."

"But on the wrong side for your argument, seeing the relation between God and the poorest creature is infinitely closer than that between any father and his child."

"Then he can't be so hard on us as the parsons say, even in the after-life?"

"He will give absolute justice, which is the only good thing. He will spare nothing to bring his children back to himself, their sole well-being, whether he achieve it here—or there. Are you satisfied with yourself, my lord?"

"No, by George!"

"You would like to be better?"

"I would."

"Then you are of the same mind with God."

The Fisherman's Lady, p. 262

I will put my laws into their mind, and write them in their hearts: and I will be to them a God, and they shall be to me a people.
Hebrews 8:10

IT MAY BE THE LORD HIMSELF

GIBBIE STOOD MOTIONLESS IN THE MIDDLE of the floor, smiling his innocent smile, asking for nothing, hinting at nothing, but resting his wild-calm eyes, with a sense of safety and mother-presence, upon the thoughtful face of the gazing woman. Her awe deepened. Involuntarily she bowed her head and, stepping to him, took him by the hand and led him to the stool she had left. There she made him sit while she brought forward her table, white with scrubbing. Then taking from a hole in the wall a platter of oatcakes, she set it upon the table. She next carried a wooden bowl through a whitewashed door to her dairy in the rock, and bringing it back filled, half with cream, half with milk, set that also on the table. Then she placed a chair before it and said, "Sit down and eat. If you were the Lord himself, my bonny man—and for all I know you may be—I could give you nothing better. It's all I have to offer."

The Baronet's Song, p. 43

And whosoever shall give to drink unto one of
these little ones a cup of cold water only in the
name of a disciple, verily I say unto you, he
shall in no wise lose his reward.
Matthew 10:42

THE GREATEST WORK—THAT DONE WITH THE HANDS

"I WOULD SEE THE POET EARN HIS BREAD BY the sweat of his brow—with his hands feed his body, and with his heart and brain feed the hearts of his brothers and sisters. Your father and I have talked a great deal about this. It is one of the meanest and silliest articles in the social creed of our country that a man is not a gentleman who works with his hands. He who would be a better gentleman than the Carpenter of Nazareth is not worthy of him. He gave up his work with his hands only to do better work for his brothers and sisters, and then he let the men and women, but mostly, I suspect, the women, that loved him support him! Thousands of young men think it more gentlemanly to be clerks than carpenters; but, if I were a man, I would rather make anything than add up figures or handle money or copy letters all day long! If I had brothers, I would ten times rather see them masons, or carpenters, or bookbinders, or gardeners, or shoemakers than have them doing what ought to be left for the weaker and more delicate!"

"Which would you like to see me, Molly—a carpenter or a shoemaker?"

"Neither of those, but I think rather a farmer, Walter. Surely you don't want to be a finer gentleman than your father! If you ask me, you couldn't do better than to stay at home and help him, and grow strong. Plough and cart, plant and harvest, and do the work of a laboring man. Nature will be your mate in her own workshop!"

What wisdom had not obedience borne in Molly! If Burns had but kept to his plough and his fields, to the birds and the beasts, to the storms and the sunshine! He was a free man while he lived by his labor among his own people. Ambition makes of gentlemen time-servers and paltry politicians. Of the ploughman-poet Burns it made an exciseman, after which his poetry was never the same!

"What will then become of the think-time you say I should have?"

"While you work with your hands, your mind will fill itself with pure and true thoughts. And knowing your father, he will allow you time to pursue your dreams. In winter, which you say is the season for poetry, there will be plenty of time, and in summer there will be some. Not a stroke of your pen will have to go for a dinner or a pair of shoes! Thoughts born of the heaven and the earth and the fountains of water will spring up in your soul and have time to ripen. If you find you are not wanted for an author, you will thank God you are not an author." *The Poet's Homecoming, pp. 183–184*

And let the beauty of the Lord our God be upon us: and establish thou the work of our hands upon us; yea, the work of our hands establish thou it.
Psalm 90:17

WHAT IS THE VERY BEGINNING?

"DAVIE," HE SAID, "HOW DO YOU FANCY THE first lesson in the New Testament ought to begin?"

"At the beginning," answered Davie, who had by this time learned to answer a question directly.

"Well, there was one who said, 'I am the beginning and the end, the first and the last'; and who can there be to begin about but him? All the New Testament is about him. A great many years ago there appeared in the world men who said that a certain man had been their companion for some time and had just left them; that he was killed by cruel men, and buried by his friends; but, as he had told them before, he would lie in the grave only three days, and rise from it on the third; and after a good while, during which they saw him several times, went up into the sky, and disappeared. It isn't a very likely story, is it?"

"No," replied Davie.

"But, Davie," Donal went on, "however unlikely it must have seemed to those who heard it, when you come to know the kind of man of whom they told it, you will see nothing could be more suitable than just what they said. And, Davie, I believe every word of it."

The Shepherd's Castle, pp. 58–59

These things have I written unto you that
believe on the name of the Son of God; that ye
may know that ye have eternal life, and that
ye may believe on the name of the Son of God.
1 John 5:13

DON'T BE ASHAMED TO BE LAST

AT LENGTH THE DAY ARRIVED TO PUT THE sickle to the barley, to be followed by the scythe in the oats. And then came the joy of labor. Books were thrown utterly aside. Everything was abandoned for the harvest field. For even when there was no fear of a change in the weather to urge labor on into the night, there was weariness enough in the work of the day to prevent the reading of anything that necessitated mental labor.

Jeanette and Margaret took to the reaping hook. The laird was in the fields from morning to night, and the boys would not stay behind. Hugh, though he was quite helpless at the sickle, thought he could wield the scythe and so joined the harvest. It was desperate work for him for a while, and he lagged far behind the others. But seeing the tutor dropping behind, David, who was the best scythe in the whole countryside, put more power into his arm, finished his first row and brought up the remainder of Hugh's before the others had done sharpening their scythes for the next.

"Be careful not to push yourself too fast," David warned him. "You'll be up with the best of them in a day or two. Take a good sweep with the scythe and let its weight pull right through the straw, and don't be at all ashamed to be last."   *The Tutor's First Love, p. 27*

But many that are first shall be last;
and the last shall be first.
Matthew 19:30

THE RIGHT TO EXERCISE AUTHORITY

THE CHAMPION OF OPPRESSED ANIMALITY soon recovered speech. "Get off the poor creature's head instantly," she said with dignified command. "I will permit no such usage of a living thing on my ground."

"I am very sorry to seem rude, my lady," answered Malcolm, "but to obey you might be to ruin my mistress' property. If the mare were to break away, she would dash herself to pieces in the wood."

"You have goaded her to madness."

"I am the more bound to take care of her, then," said Malcolm. "But indeed it is only temper—such temper, however, that I almost believe she is at times possessed of a demon."

"The demon is in yourself. There is none in her but what your cruelty has put there. Let her up, I command you."

"I dare not, my lady. If she were to get loose, she would tear your ladyship to pieces."

"I will take my chance."

"But I will not, my lady. I know the danger and have to take care of you who do not. There is no occasion to be uneasy about the mare. She is tolerably comfortable. I am not hurting her—not much. Your ladyship does not reflect how strong a horse's skull is. And you see what great powerful breaths she draws."

"She is in agony!" cried Clementina.

"Not in the least, my lady. She is only balked of her own way and does not like it."

"And what right have you to balk her of her own way? Has she no right to a mind of her own?"

"She may of course have her mind, but she can't have her way. She has got a master."

"And what right have you to be her master?"

"That my master, my Lord Lossie, gave me charge of her."

"I don't mean that sort of right. That goes for nothing. What right in the nature of things can you have to tyrannize over any creature?"

"None, my lady. But the higher nature has the right to rule the lower in righteousness. Even you can't have your own way always, my lady."

"I certainly cannot now, so long as you keep in that position. Pray, is it in virtue of your being the higher nature that you keep *my* way from me?"

"No, my lady. But it is in virtue of right. If I wanted to take your ladyship's property, your dogs would be justified in refusing me my way. I do not think I exaggerate when I say that if my mare here had *her* way, there would not be a living creature about your house by this day next week."   *The Marquis' Secret, pp. 90–91*

And God said, Let us make man in our image,
after our likeness: and let them have dominion
over the fish of the sea, and over the fowl of
the air, and over the cattle, and over all the
earth, and over every creeping thing that
creepeth upon the earth.
Genesis 1:26

THE PERFECT IDEA OF LIFE IS GOD

"TO TELL YOU THE TRUTH, I DO NOT MUCH care to argue the point with you. It is by no means a matter of the *first* importance whether we live forever or not."

"Mr. Polwarth!" exclaimed the draper.

The gatekeeper smiled what might have been called a knowing smile.

"Suppose a thing were in itself not worth having," he went on, "would it be the gift to give it to someone forever? Most people think it a fine thing to have a bit of land to call their own and leave to their children. But suppose it was a stinking and undrainable swamp, full of foul springs?"

"You astonish me!" exclaimed Mr. Drew, recovering his mental breath. "How can you compare God's gift to such a horrible thing? Where would we be without eternal life?"

"Mr. Drew," said Polwarth half merrily, "are you going to help me drag my chain out to its weary length, or are you too much shocked at the doubtful condition of its first links to touch them? I promise you the last shall be of bright gold."

"I beg your pardon," said the draper, "I might have known you didn't mean it."

"On the contrary, I mean everything I say. Perhaps I don't mean everything you fancy I mean. Tell me, would life be worth having on any and every possible condition?"

"Certainly not."

"You know some, I dare say, who would be glad to be rid of life such as it is, and such as they suppose it must continue?"

"Occasionally you meet someone like that."

"I repeat then, that to prove life endless is not a matter of the world's *first* importance. It follows that there is something of prior importance, and greater importance, than the possession of mere immortality. What do you suppose that something is?"

"I imagine that the immortality itself should be worth possessing," reasoned the draper.

"Yes, if the life should be of such quality that one could enjoy it forever. And what if it is not?"

"The question then would be whether or not it could not be made such."

"You are right. And wherein consists the essential inherent worthiness of a life as life? The only perfect idea of life is God, the only one. That a man should complete himself by taking into himself that origin, and with his whole being commit himself to will the will of God in himself—that is the highest possible condition of a man. Then he has completed his cycle. This is the essence of life—the rounding, creating, unifying of the man.

"The man with life so in himself—that quality of life we spoke of—will not dream of asking whether he shall live forever. It is only in the twilight of a half life that the doubtful anxiety of immortality can arise."

The Curate's Awakening, pp. 179–180

So when this corruptible shall have put on
incorruption, and this mortal shall have put
on immortality, then shall be brought to pass
the saying that is written, Death is
swallowed up in victory.
1 Corinthians 15:54

A HARVEST OF LOVE AS WELL AS GRAIN

AT LENGTH THE OATS AND WHEAT AND barley were gathered in all over the valley of the two rivers. The master returned from the seacoast, bringing Truffey, radiant with life, with him. Nothing could lengthen that shrunken limb, but in the other and the crutch together he had more than the function of the two.

The master was his idol, and the master was a happier man. The scene of his late failure had begun to fade a little from his brain. He had been loving and helping; and the love and help had turned into a great joy, whose tide washed from out of his heart the bitterness of his remembered sin. When we love God and man truly, all the guilt and oppression of past sin will be swept away.

So the earth and all that was in it did the master good. And he came back able to look the people in the face—humble still, but no longer humiliated. And when the children gathered again on a Monday morning with the sad feeling that the holidays were over, the master's prayer was different from what it used to be, and the work was not so bad as before, and school was not so hateful after all. *The Maiden's Bequest, p. 190*

No man hath seen God at any time. If we love one another, God dwelleth in us, and his love is perfected in us.
1 John 4:12

THE HIGHEST MEANS OF SPIRITUAL EDUCATION

"WILL YOU BE AT CHURCH TOMORROW?" asked Wingfold.

"That will depend on you: would you rather have me there or not?"

"A thousand times rather," answered the curate. "To have one man there who knows what I mean is to have a double dose of courage. But I came tonight mainly to tell you something else. I have been greatly puzzled this last week about how I ought to regard the Bible—I mean as to its inspiration. What am I to say about it?"

"Those are two very distinct things. Why do you want to say something about it before you have anything to say? For yourself, however, let me just ask if you have not already found in that book the highest means of spiritual education and development you have yet met with? It is the man Christ Jesus we have to know, and the Bible we must use to that end—not for theory or dogma. In that light, it is the most practical and useful book in the world." *The Curate's Awakening, p. 91*

And this is life eternal, that they might know
thee the only true God, and Jesus Christ,
whom thou hast sent.
John 17:3

49

You've Got to Repent

THE OLD MAN STOPPED IN HIS WALK, turned, and faced his son.

"Father," repeated Robert, "you've got to repent, and God won't let you off, and you needn't think he will. You'll have to repent someday."

"In hell, Robert," said Andrew, looking him full in the eyes, as he had never looked at him before. It seemed as if even so much acknowledgment of the truth had already made him bolder and more honest.

"Yes. Either on earth or in hell. Would it not be better on earth?"

"But it will be no use in hell," he murmured.

In those few words lay the germ of the preference for hell of poor souls, enfeebled by wickedness. They will not have to *do* anything there, only to moan and cry and suffer forever, they think. It is not so much the sorrow or remorse of repentance they dread; it is the action it involves; it is the having to be different, behave differently, that they shrink from. And they have been taught to believe that this will not be required of them there; that their wills will not be called into action. But tell them that the fire of God, both around them and within them, *will* compel them; that the vision of an open door beyond the smoke and the flames will ever urge them to call up the ice-bound will that it may obey, that the torturing spirit of God in them *will* keep their consciences awake—not to remind them of what they ought to have done, but to tell them what they *must* do now—and hell will lose its unnatural fascination for them. Tell them that there is *no* refuge from the compelling love of

God, except that love itself, that if they make their bed in hell, they shall not escape him; and then, perhaps, they will have some true perceptions of the fire that is not quenched.

"Father, it *will* be of use in hell," said Robert. "God will give you no rest even there. You will have to repent someday, I do believe—if not now under the sunshine of heaven, then in the torture of the awful world where there is no light but that of the conscience. Would it not be better and easier to repent now, with your wife waiting for you in heaven, and your mother waiting for you on earth?"

The Musician's Quest, pp. 250–251

For it is written, As I live, saith the Lord,
every knee shall bow to me, and every
tongue shall confess to God.
Romans 14:11

This is and has been the Father's work from the beginning—to bring us into the home of his heart, where he shares the glories of life with the Living One, in whom was born life to light men back to the original life.

This is our destiny. And however one may refuse, he will find it hard to fight with God—useless to kick against the goads of his love. For the Father is goading him, or will goad him, if need be, into life by unrest and trouble. Even the fire of hell will have its turn if less will not do.

Knowing the Heart of God, p. 46;
Unspoken Sermons, Second Series—"The Truth in Jesus"

BETTER NO GOD THAN A WRONG GOD

IT IS HARD TO UNDERSTAND HOW A MAN can prefer being the slave of blind helpless law to being the child of living Wisdom, why he would believe in nothing rather than a perfect Will. Yet it is not unintelligible because he cannot see the Wisdom or the Will unless he draws near to it.

But for those who have lost a "faith" they once adhered to in their youth, for my part I would rather disbelieve with them than have what they have lost. For I would rather have no God than the God whom they suppose me to believe in, and therefore must be the God in whom they imagined they believed in in the days of their ignorance. That those were the days of their ignorance, I do not doubt; but are these the days of their knowledge? The time will come when they will see deeper into their own hearts than now, and will be humbled, like many other men, by what they see.

The Lady's Confession, pp. 68–69

*Because thine heart was tender, and thou didst
humble thyself before God, when thou
heardest his words against this place, and
against the inhabitants thereof, and
humbledst thyself before me, and didst rend
thy clothes, and weep before me; I have even
heard thee also, saith the Lord.*
2 Chronicles 34:27

THE "TEACHING" OF RELIGION IS NOT ALWAYS NECESSARY

SHE HAD NEVER BEEN TAUGHT ANY RELIGION, but from her earliest recollection she had the feeling of a Presence. The sky over her head brought it, as did any horizon far or near. But when she went to church, none of the Presence came near her. She had no idea of ever having done wrong, no feeling that God was pleased or displeased with her, or had any occasion to be either. She did not know that the feeling of the Presence came near her in her horse, in her dog, and in the people about her. He came nearer in a thunderstorm, a moonlit night, a sweet wind—anything that woke the sense of the old freedom of her childhood. She felt the presence then, but never knew it as a Presence.

Neither did she know that there was a place where that Presence was always awaiting her—a place called in a certain old book "thy closet." She did not know that there opened the one horizon—infinitely far, yet near as her own heart. But he is there for those that seek him, not for those who do not look for him. Until they do, all he can do is to make them feel the want of him. Barbara had not begun to seek him. She did not know there was anybody to seek: she only missed him without knowing what she missed.   *The Baron's Apprenticeship, p. 53*

*Whither shall I go from thy spirit? or whither
shall I flee from thy presence?*
Psalm 139:7

DO YOU REALLY BELIEVE ALL THAT MOONSHINE?

"YOU THINK GOD HEARS PRAYERS—DO you?"

"I do."

"Then I wish you would ask him to let me off—I mean, to let me die right out when I do die. What's the good of making a body miserable?"

"I am sure it would be of no use to pray that. He certainly will not throw away a thing he has made because that thing may be foolish enough to prefer the dust-hole to a cabinet."

"Wouldn't you do it now, if I asked you?"

"What—let you off, let you die and that be the end?"

"Yes, surely *you* would not torture me."

"I would do nothing but what God will do, which is always the best. I would leave you in God's hands rather than inside the gate of heaven."

"I don't understand you. You wouldn't say such a thing if you cared for me! Only, why should you care for me?"

"I would give my life for you."

"Come, now! Bosh! I don't believe that!"

"Why, I wouldn't be a Christian if I wouldn't."

"You are being downright absurd!" he cried. But the look on his face did not seem exactly as if he thought it.

"Absurd!" repeated Mary. "Isn't that what makes him our Savior? How could I be his disciple if I wouldn't do as he did?"

"You are saying a good deal."

"But to follow Jesus, I have no choice."

"I wouldn't do that for anybody under the sun."

"You are not his disciple. You have not been going about life with him."

"And you have?"

"Yes—for many years. Besides, I cannot help thinking there is one for whom you would do it."

"If you mean my wife, you were never more mistaken. I would do nothing of the sort."

"I did not mean your wife, I mean Jesus Christ."

"Oh, I dare say! Well, perhaps, if I knew him as you do, and if I were quite sure he wanted it done for him."

"He does want it done for him—always and every day—not for his own sake, though it does make him very glad. To give up your way for his is to die for him. And when any one will do that, then he is able to do everything for him. For then, and not until then, he gets such a hold of him that he can lift him up, and set him down beside himself. That's how my father used to teach me, and now I see it for myself to be true."

"It's all very grand, no doubt. But it's nowhere, you know. It's all in your own head, and nowhere else. You don't, you can't possibly believe all that moonshine!"

"I believe it so thoroughly that I live in the strength and hope it gives me, and order my ways according to it every day in everything I do. At least I try to do so."

A Daughter's Devotion, pp. 282–283

*Hereby perceive we the love of God, because
he laid down his life for us: and we ought to
lay down our lives for the brethren.*

1 John 3:16

TO BE OF THE TRUTH

IT WAS NOT HER DESIRE TO SEE HIM "converted"; indeed, the word would have had little meaning to Barbara. Certain attempts at what is called conversion are but manifestations of greed for power over others; swellings of the ambition to propagate one's own creed and proselytize victoriously; hungerings to see self reflected in another convinced.

In such efforts lie dangers as vulgar as the minds that make them, and love the excitement of them. But genuine love is far beyond such groveling delights.

Barbara was one who, so far as human eyes could see, had never required conversion. She had but to go on, recognize, and do. She turned to the light by a holy will as well as holy instinct. She needed much instruction, and might yet have fierce battles to fight, but to convert such as Barbara must be to turn them the wrong way; for the whole energy of her being was in the direction of what was right. She needed but to be told a good thing—not *told that a thing was good*—and at once she received it—that is, obeyed it, the only way of receiving a truth. She responded immediately upon every reception of light, every expansion of true knowledge.

She was essentially *of* the truth; therefore when she came into relation with such a soul as Wingfold, a soul so much more developed than herself, her life was fed from his and began to grow faster. For he taught her to know the eternal Man who bore witness to her Father, and Barbara became his child, the inheritor of the universe. Fortunately, her life had not been loaded to the ground with what is generally regarded as a *religious education*. Such teaching is the mother of more tears in humble souls, and more presumption in the proud and selfish,

than perhaps any other influence out of whose darkness God brings light. Neither ascetic nor mystic nor doctrinist of any sort, caring nothing for church or chapel or observance of any kind for its own sake, Barbara believed in God, and was coming to believe in Jesus Christ. And glad she was as she had never been before that there was such a person as Jesus Christ!

Wingfold never sought to influence her in any way concerning her workman-friend; he only sought to strengthen her in the truth.

The Baron's Apprenticeship, pp. 133—134

But he that doeth truth cometh to the light, that his deeds may be made manifest, that they are wrought in God.
John 3:21

The things most urgent to be done, those which lie not at the door but on the very table of a person's mind, are the things most often neglected, let alone, and postponed.

If the Lord of life demands high virtue of us, can it be that he does not care for the first principles of justice? May a person become strong in righteousness without learning to speak the truth to his neighbor? Shall one climb the last flight of the stairs who has never set foot on the first?

Truth is one. He who is faithful in the small thing at hand is of the truth. He who will only do the great thing, who postpones the small thing at hand for the sake of the great thing farther from him, is not of the truth.   *Knowing the Heart of God, p. 82;*
Unspoken Sermons, Second Series—"The Cause of Spiritual Stupidity"

A Son's Prayer

Ian said to himself, "I must go away. I am only paining her. She will come to see things better without me. I will go, and come again."

His heart broke forth in prayer.

"O God, let my mother see that you are indeed true-hearted; that you do not give us life by bits and pieces but abundantly; that you do not make men in order to assert your dominion over them, but that they may partake of your life. O God, have pity on me when I cannot understand, and teach me as you would a little earthly son you would carry in your arms. When pride rises in me and I feel as if I ought to walk about without your hand, then think of me and I shall know that I cannot live or think without your self-willing life. Help me to know that I am because you are, that I have no wisdom or insight of my own, that all life exists because you have breathed your being into it. Without your eternity in us, we are so small that we think ourselves great, and are thus miserably contemptible. You alone are true! Make me and my brother strong to be the very men you would have us, as your brothers, Christ, the children of your Father. You are our perfect brother—perfect in love, in courage, in tenderness. Amen, Lord! I am yours!"

The Highlander's Last Song, p. 87

*He that speaketh of himself seeketh his own
glory: but he that seeketh his glory that sent
him, the same is true, and no unrighteousness
is in him.*
John 7:18

GOD SOMETIMES SHINES IN SIDEWAYS

HESTER SAID NOTHING FURTHER, BUT still caught only a glimpse of the doctor's meaning. We are surrounded with things difficult to understand, and the way most people take it is to look away lest they should find out they have to understand them. Hester suspected skepticism in his remarks: most doctors, she believed, leaned in that direction. But she herself had begun to have a true notion of serving man. Therefore, there was no fear of her not coming to see, sooner or later, what serving God meant. She did serve him, so she could not fail to discover the word that belonged to the act: only by serving can one discover what serving him means. Some people are constantly rubbing at their sky-lights, but if they do not keep their other windows clean also, there will not be much light in the house. God, like his body, the light, is all about us, and prefers to shine in upon us sideways, for we could not endure the power of his vertical glory. No mortal man can see God and live, and he who does not love his brother whom he has seen will not love his God whom he has not seen. He will come to us in the morning through the eyes of a child when we have been gazing all night at the stars in vain.

The Gentlewoman's Choice, pp. 53–54

If a man say, I love God, and hateth his
brother, he is a liar: for he that loveth not his
brother whom he hath seen, how can he love
God whom he hath not seen?
1 John 4:20

THE BUSINESS OF LIFE IS DOING GOD'S THINGS

MOLLY WAS ONE OF THE WISE WOMEN of this world—and thus, thoughts grew for her first out of things, and not things out of thoughts. God's things come out of his thoughts; our realities are God's thoughts made manifest in things, and out of them our thoughts must come. Then the things that come out of our thoughts will be real. Neither our own fancies nor the judgments of the world must be the ground of our theories or behavior.

This, at least, was Molly's working theory of life. She saw plainly that her business—every day, every hour, every moment—was to order her way as he who had sent her into being would have her order her way. Doing God's things—that is, what God gave her to do—God's thoughts would come to her. God's things were better than man's thoughts, man's best thoughts the discovery of the thoughts hidden in God's things. Obeying him, perhaps a day would come in which God would think directly into the mind of his child without the intervention of things!

For Molly had made the one rational, one practical discovery of being—that life is to be lived, not by helpless assent or aimless drifting, but by active cooperation with the Life that has said Live. To her everything was part of a whole, which, with its parts, she was learning to know. She was finding out the secrets of life by obedience to what she already knew. There is nothing like obedience—that is, duty done—for developing even

the common intellect. Those who obey are soon wiser than all their lessons, while from those who do not obey, even what knowledge they started with will be taken away. *The Poet's Homecoming, pp. 169–170*

Woe unto you, lawyers! for ye have taken away the key of knowledge: ye entered not in yourselves, and them that were entering in ye hindered.
Luke 11:52

I will enter no debate for or against mere doctrine. I have no desire to change the opinion of man or woman. Let the Lord himself teach them. A man who does not have the mind of Christ—and no man can have the mind of Christ except him who makes it his business to obey him—cannot have correct opinions concerning him. Our business is not to think correctly, but to live truly. Then first will there be a possibility of our thinking correctly.

Discovering the Character of God, p. 250;
Unspoken Sermons, Third Series—"Justice"

ESSENTIAL LADYHOOD

THINGS WENT ON IN THE SAME WAY FOR four years more, the only visible change being that Kirsty seldom went about barefooted.

She was now between twenty-two and twenty-three. Her face, whose ordinary expression had always been quiet, was now in general quieter still. But when heart or soul was moved, it would flash and glow as only such a face could. Live revelation of deeps rarely rippled except by the breath of God: how could it but grow more beautiful! Cloud or shadow of cloud was hardly to be seen upon it.

Her mother, much younger than her father, was still well and strong, and Kirsty, still not much needed at home, continued to spend the greater part of her time with her brother and her books. As to her person, she was now in the first flower of harmonious womanly strength. Nature had indeed done what it could to make her a lady, but nature was not her mother, and Kirsty's essential ladyhood came from higher up, namely from the Source itself of nature. Simple truth was its crown, and grace was the garment of it. To see her walk or run was to look on the divine idea of motion.

The Peasant Girl's Dream, p. 91

And the Word was made flesh, and dwelt among us, (and we beheld his glory, the glory as of the only begotten of the Father,) full of grace and truth.
John 1:14

THE POWER OF SIMPLE BELIEF

THE WORLD LITTLE KNOWS WHAT A POWER among men is he who simply and thoroughly believes in him who is Lord of the world to save men from their sins! He may be neither wise nor prudent in the world's eyes. He may be clothed in no attractive colors or in any word of power. And yet if he has but that love for his neighbor that is rooted in and springs from love to his God, he is always a redeeming, reconciling influence among his fellows. The Robertsons were genial of heart, loving and tender toward man or woman in need of them, and their door was always open for such to enter and find help. If the parson insisted on the wrath of God against sin, he did not fail to give assurance of the Lord's tenderness toward such that had fallen.

Together the godly pair at length persuaded Isobel of the eager forgiveness of the Son of Man. They assured her that he could not drive from him the very worst of sinners, but loved—nothing less than tenderly loved—anyone who turned his face to the Father. She would no doubt, they said, have to bear her trespass in the eyes of the unforgiving who looked upon her, but the Lord would lift her high and welcome her to the home of the glad-hearted.
The Minister's Restoration, p. 105

And what is the exceeding greatness of his power to us-ward who believe, according to the working of his mighty power.
Ephesians 1:19

WE MUST GIVE UP THIS WORLD'S TREASURE

ALL AT ONCE HE WOKE WITH A START AND a cry, but found it safe in both his hands.

"You didn't try to take the cup from me—did you, Dawtie!"

"No, sir," answered Dawtie. "I would never take it out of your hand, but I *would* be glad to take it out of your heart."

"If only they would bury it with me!" he murmured, heedless of her words.

"Oh, sir! Do you want it burning your heart to all eternity? Give it up, laird, and take instead the treasure that no thief can ever steal."

"Yes, Dawtie, yes! That is the true treasure!"

"And to get it we must sell all we have."

"He gives and withholds as he sees fit."

"No, laird. To get that treasure we must give up this world's."

"I'll not believe it!"

"And then when you go down in blackness, longing for the cup that you will never see again, you will complain that God would not give you the strength to fling it from you?"

He hugged the chalice as he replied. "Fling it from me!" he cried fiercely. "Girl, who are you to torment me before my time?"

"God gives every man and woman the power to do what he requires, and we are fearfully to blame for not using the strength God gives us."

"I cannot bear the strain of thinking!" gasped the laird.

"Then give up thinking, and do the thing! Or shall I take it for you?"

She held out her hand as she spoke.

"No! No!" he cried, grasping the cup tighter. "You shall not touch it! You would give it to the earl! I know you! Saints hate what is beautiful!"

"I like better to look at things in my Father's hand than in my own."

"You want to see my cup—it *is* my cup!—in the hands of that spendthrift fool, Lord Borland!"

"It is in the Father's hand, whoever has it."

The Landlady's Master, p. 156

*And a certain ruler asked him, saying, Good
Master, what shall I do to inherit eternal life?
And Jesus said unto him, Why callest thou
me good? none is good, save one, that is, God.
Thou knowest the commandments, Do not
commit adultery, Do not kill, Do not steal,
Do not bear false witness, Honour thy father
and thy mother. And he said, All these have I
kept from my youth up. Now when Jesus
heard these things, he said unto him, Yet
lackest thou one thing: sell all that thou hast,
and distribute unto the poor, and thou shalt
have treasure in heaven: and come, follow me.
And when he heard this, he was very
sorrowful: for he was very rich. And when
Jesus saw that he was very sorrowful, he
said, How hardly shall they that have riches
enter into the kingdom of God!*

Luke 18:18–24

WHAT THE WORLD CALLS FINE IS THE DEVIL'S TOOL

AS THEY TALKED, MARY WAS GIVING HER final touches to the arrangement. When she was done she searched Hesper's jewelry box and found a fine bracelet of the true, Oriental topaz: this she clasped upon one arm. Then she took off all the rings Hesper had just put on except a certain glorious sapphire, and then led her again to the mirror. If there, Hesper was far more pleased with herself than was reasonable or lovely, my reader need not therefore fear a sermon from the text, "Beauty is only skin-deep," for that text is out of the devil's Bible. No, the maker of all beauty is the same One who made the seven stars, and his works are past finding out. But the woman's share in her own beauty may be infinitely less than skin-deep; and there is but one greater fool than the man who worships that beauty—that is the woman who prides herself upon it, as if she were the fashioner and to the thing fashioned.

But poor Hesper had much excuse, though not justification. She had had many of the disadvantages, and hardly a single one of the benefits of poverty. She had heard constantly from childhood the most worldly and greedy talk, the commonest expression of dependence on the favors of Mammon, and thus had from the first been prepared to marry money. She had been taught no other way of doing her part to procure the things of which the Father knows we have need. She had never earned a dinner, had never done or thought of doing a day's work—of offering the world anything. She had

never dreamed of being any use, even to herself. Out of it all, she had brought but the knowledge that this beauty with which she was chanced to be blessed was worth much in the world—was worth everything, in fact, the world calls fine, and the devil offers to those who, unscarred by his inherent ugliness, will fall down and worship him. *A Daughter's Devotion, p. 179*

Favour is deceitful, and beauty is vain: but a
woman that feareth the Lord,
she shall be praised.
Proverbs 31:30

We must not merely do as he did, we must see things as he saw them, regard them as he regarded them. We must take the will of God as the very life of our being. We must neither try to get our own way, nor trouble ourselves as to what may be thought or said of us.

The world must be to us as nothing.

I would not be misunderstood if I may avoid it. When I say *the world*, I do not mean the world God makes and means. Even less do I mean the human hearts that live in that world. Rather I mean the world man makes by choosing the perversion of his own nature—a world apart from and opposed to God's world.

Knowing the Heart of God, p. 115;
Unspoken Sermons, Second Series—"Self Denial"

WHO IS REALLY FREE?

HE RAN HE KNEW NOT WHITHER, FEELING nothing but the desire first to get into some covert and then to run farther. His first rush was for the shrubbery, his next across the little park to the wood beyond. He did not feel the wind of his running on his bare skin. He did not feel the hunger that had made him so unable to bear the lash. On and on he ran. At length he came where a high wall joining some water formed a boundary. The water was a brook from the mountain, here widening and deepening into a still pool. He threw himself in and swam straight across; ever after that, swimming seemed to him as natural as walking.

Then first awoke a faint sense of safety; for on the other side he was knee deep in heather. He was on the wild hill, with miles on miles of cover! He would get right into the heather and lie with it all around and over him till the night came. Where he would go then he did not know. But it was all one, he could go anywhere. Donal must mind his cows, and the men must mind the horses, and Mistress Jean must mind her kitchen, but Sir Gibbie could go where he pleased.

The Baronet's Song, p. 71

If the Son therefore shall make you free,
ye shall be free indeed.
John 8:36

A COUNTRY ROBED IN THE COLORS OF AUTUMN

WE FOUND ROOMS IN A FARMHOUSE ON THE topmost part of the hill. After an early dinner we went out for a walk. But we did not go far before we sat down upon the grass. Robert laid himself at full length and gazed upward.

"When I look like this into the blue sky," he said after a moment's silence, "it seems so deep and so peaceful that I could lie for centuries and wait for the dawning of the face of God in his awful lovingkindness."

I had never heard Falconer talk of his own feelings like this, but glancing at the face of his father I saw at once that it was for his sake that he had said it. The old man had thrown himself back too, and was gazing into the sky, puzzling himself to comprehend what his son could mean. I fear he concluded that Robert was lacking in common sense and that too much religion had made him a dreamer and a mystic. A mystic Falconer certainly was, but not as his father thought. Still, I thought I could see a kind of awe pass like a spiritual shadow across his face. No one can detect the first beginnings of any life.

The Musician's Quest, p. 254

Awake to righteousness, and sin not.
1 Corinthians 15:34

THERE IS ALWAYS TIME TO BEGIN AGAIN

"IT WON'T DO TO SAY THAT I SHOULD LIKE to be, I must be, and that's not so easy. It's too hard to be good. I would have to fight for it, but there's no time. How is a poor devil to get out of such an infernal scrape?"

"Keep the Commandments."

"That's it, of course. But there's no time, I tell you— no time! At least that's what those cursed doctors will keep telling me."

"If there were but time to draw another breath, there would be time to begin."

"How am I to begin? Which am I to begin with?"

"There is one commandment that includes all the rest."

"Which is that?"

"To believe in the Lord Jesus Christ."

"That's cant!"

"After thirty years' trial of it, it is to me the essence of wisdom. It has given me a peace which makes life or death all but indifferent to me."

"What am I to believe about him, then?"

"You are to believe *in* him, not *about* him."

"I don't understand."

"He is our Lord and Master, Elder Brother, King, Savior, the Divine Man, the human God. To believe in him is to give ourselves up to him in obedience—to search out his will and do it."

"But there's no time, I tell you," the marquis almost shrieked.

"And I tell you there is all eternity to do it in. Take him for your Master, and he will demand nothing of you

which you are not able to perform. This is the open door to bliss. With your last breath you can cry to him, and he will hear you as he heard the thief on the cross. It makes my heart swell to think about it. No cross-questioning of the poor fellow, no preaching to him. He just took him with him where he was going, to make a man of him."   *The Fisherman's Lady, pp. 262–263*

Behold, now is the accepted time; behold,
now is the day of salvation.
2 Corinthians 6:2

To every soul dissatisfied with itself, this rousing and consoling word comes from the Power that lives and makes him live—that in his hungering and thirsting he is blessed, for he shall be filled. The more he hungers and thirsts the more blessed is he; the more room there is in him to receive that which God is yet more eager to give than he is to have.

It is the miserable emptiness that makes a man hunger and thirst. And, as the body hungers and thirsts for food and drink, so the soul hungers and thirsts after righteousness because the man's nature needs it—needs righteousness because he was made for it; and the soul desires its own. Man's nature is good, and desires more good. Therefore, no one need be discouraged because he is empty of good, for what is emptiness but room to be filled? Emptiness is need of good. And the emptiness that desires good is itself good.

Knowing the Heart of God, p. 163;
The Hope of the Gospel—"God's Family"

DOING IS GREATER THAN HAVING

SHE WAS IN DANGER OF THINKING A WORKING man's poverty contained some essential goodness in and of itself, not realizing that, in general, the working man is just as foolish and unfit as the rich man. It is not whether a man be rich or poor that matters, but of what kind of stuff he is made.

In fact, the poor man gives the rich man his control over him by cherishing the same feelings as the rich man concerning riches, by fancying the rich man a greater man, and longing to be rich like him. A man that can *do* things is greater than any man who only *has* things.

The Baron's Apprenticeship, p. 77

O Lord, are not thine eyes upon the truth?
thou hast stricken them, but they have not
grieved; thou hast consumed them, but they
have refused to receive correction: they have
made their faces harder than a rock; they
have refused to return. Therefore I said,
Surely these are poor; they are foolish: for
they know not the way of the Lord,
nor the judgment of their God.
Jeremiah 5:3—4

MANY DO NOT SEE THE SHELL THAT IMPRISONS THEM

THE NIGHT WAS CLEAR AND THE TWO walked for some time in silence. It was a sudden change from the low barn, the dull candles, and the excitement of the dance, to the awful space, the clear pure far-off lights, and the great stillness. Both felt it, though differently; both of them sought after peace. Mercy was only beginning to seek it, not knowing what she needed. Ian sought it in silence with God; she in relation with others of her kind. She was a human chicken that had begun to be aware of herself, but had not yet attacked the shell that enclosed her. Because it was transparent and she could see life about her, she did not know that she was in a shell, or that if she did not exercise the might of her own life, she was sealing herself up to death. Many who think themselves free have never yet even seen the shell that imprisons them—know nothing of the liberty the Lord of life wants to give them. Men and women fight many a phantom when they ought to be chipping at their shells. They think they are getting on in the world, when the world is but their shell, killing the infant Christ who houses with them. *The Highlander's Last Song, p. 94*

Stand fast therefore in the liberty wherewith
Christ hath made us free, and be not
entangled again with the yoke of bondage.
Galatians 5:1

TO BE WHAT WE
WERE MADE FOR

"BUT YOU MUST ALLOW THAT SOME THINGS are lost!" said Miss Carmichael.

"Yes, surely!" answered Donal. "Why else should he have to come and look for them till he find them?"

This was hardly such an answer as the theologian had expected, and she was not immediately ready with her rejoinder.

"But some of them are lost after all!" she finally murmured.

"Doubtless," replied Donal. "Some of his sheep run away again. But he goes after them again."

"Does he always?"

"Yes."

"I do not believe it."

"Then you do not believe that God is infinite?"

"Yes, I do."

"How can you? Is he not the Lord God merciful and gracious?"

"I am glad you know that."

"But if his mercy and his graciousness are not infinite, then he is not infinite."

"There are other attributes in which he is infinite."

"But he is not infinite in them all. He is not infinite in those which are the most beautiful, the most divine."

"I do not care for human argument. I go by the Word of God."

"Let me hear, then."

"There is the doctrine of adoption," she said. "Does not that teach us that God chooses to make some his children and not others?"

"God's mercy is infinite; and the doctrine of adoption is one of the falsest of all the doctrines invented by the so-called Church, and it is used by yet less loving teachers to oppress the souls of God's true children."

"You may think as you please, Mr. Grant, but while Paul teaches the doctrine, I will hold it. He may perhaps know a little better than you."

"Paul teaches no such doctrine. He teaches just what I have been saying. The Word applies it to the raising of one who is a son to the true position of a son."

"It seems to me presumptuous of you to determine what the apostle meant."

"Why, Miss Carmichael, do you think the gospel comes to us as to a set of fools? I am bound by the command of the Master to understand the things he says. He commands me to see their rectitude, because, they being true, I have to be able to see them true. Any use of a single word Paul says to oppress a human heart with the feeling that it is not the child of God comes of the devil. To fulfill the very necessities of our being, we must be his children in brain and heart, in body and soul and spirit, in obedience and hope. Then only is our creation fulfilled—then only shall we be what we were made for."

The Shepherd's Castle, pp. 142–143

And the very God of peace sanctify you
wholly; and I pray God your whole spirit
and soul and body be preserved blameless
unto the coming of our Lord Jesus Christ.
1 Thessalonians 5:23

WHAT IS A CHURCH?

"TELL ME, MR. CRAWFORD, WHAT MAKES A gathering a church?"

"It would take me some time to arrange my ideas before I could answer you," replied George, uncertain to unexpectedly find himself on the other end of the questioning.

"Is it not the presence of Christ that makes an assembly a church?"

"I suppose that is true," said George hesitantly.

"Does he not say that where two or three are met in his name, there he is in the midst of them?"

"Well?"

"Then thus far will I justify myself to you, that if I do not go to what you call *church*, yet I often make one of such company met in his name."

"He does not limit the company to two or three."

"Assuredly not. But if I find I get more help and strength with a certain few, why should I go to a gathering of a multitude to get less: Will you draw another line of definition than the Master's? Why should it be more sacred to worship with five hundred or five thousand than with three? If he is in the midst of them, they cannot be wrongly gathered."

"It looks as if you thought yourselves better than everybody else."

"I consider myself better than no man. Besides, if it were such that we thought, then certainly he would not be one of the gathering."

"How are you to know that he is in the midst of you?"

"His presence cannot be proved; it can only be known. One thing for certain, if we are not keeping his commandments, he is not among us. But if he does meet

us, it is not necessary to the joy of his presence that we should be able to prove that he is there. If a man has the company of the Lord, he will care little whether someone else does or does not believe that he has."

"Your way fosters division in the church."

"Did the Lord come to send peace on the earth? My way, as you call it, would indeed make division, but division between those who *call* themselves his, and those who *are* his. It would bring together those that love him. Company would merge with company that they might look on the Lord together. I don't believe that Jesus cares much for what is called the visible church. But he cares with his very Godhead for those who do as he tells them. They are his Father's friends. They are his elect by whom he will save the world. It is by those who obey, and by their obedience, that he will save those who do not obey, that is, will bring them to obey. It is one by one the world will pass to his side. There is no saving of the masses. If a thousand be converted at once, it is still every single lonely man that is converted."

The Landlady's Master, pp. 66–67

Suppose ye that I am come to give peace on earth? I tell you, Nay; but rather division.
Luke 12:51

No evil can be cured in mankind except by its being cured in individual men and women. There is no way of making three men right but by making right each one of the three. But a cure in one man who repents and turns is a beginning of the cure of the whole human race.   *Knowing the Heart of God, pp. 212–213;*
The Hope of the Gospel—"Salvation From Sin"

EVIL IS HARD EVEN FOR GOD TO OVERCOME

THERE ARE MANY WHO THINK TO REVERENCE the Most High by assuming that he can and should do anything or everything that pleases him in a mere moment. In their eyes power is a grander thing than love. But his Love is higher than his omnipotence. See what it cost him to redeem the world! He did not find that easy, or to be done in a moment without pain or toil. Yes, God is omnipotent—awfully omnipotent. For he wills, effects, and perfects the thing which, because of the bad in us, he has to carry out in suffering and sorrow. Evil is a hard thing, even for God to overcome. Yet thoroughly and altogether and triumphantly will he overcome it. But not by crushing it underfoot—any god of man's idea could do that!—but by conquest of heart over heart, of life over life, of life over death, of love over all. Nothing shall be too hard for God who fears not pain, but will deliver and make true and blessed at his own severest cost. *The Gentlewoman's Choice, p. 81*

Neither by the blood of goats and calves, but by his own blood he entered in once into the holy place, having obtained eternal redemption for us.
Hebrews 9:12

To Him Who Obeys Well, the Truth Comes Easy

FATHER AND SON WERE NOW SELDOM OUT of each other's sight. The capacity of the old man for taking in what was new was wonderful. Yet it was hardly to be wondered at, seeing it was the natural result of the constant practice of what he learned—for all truth understood becomes duty. To him who obeys well, the truth comes easy; to him who does not obey, it comes not at all, or comes in forms of fear and dismay. The true, that is the obedient, man cannot help seeing the truth, for it is the very business of his being—the natural concern of his soul. The religion of these two was obedience and prayer, their theories only the print of their spiritual feet as they walked homeward. *The Laird's Inheritance, p. 246*

Let us hear the conclusion of the whole matter:
Fear God, and keep his commandments: for
this is the whole duty of man.
Ecclesiastes 12:13

To *do* his words is to enter into vital relationship with Jesus; to obey him is the *only* way to be one with him. There can be no truth, no reality, in any initiation of at-one-ment with him, that is not obedience.

Knowing the Heart of God, p. 31;
Unspoken Sermons, Second Series—"The Truth in Jesus"

WE NEED NOT UNDERSTAND EVERYTHING

THE NEXT MORNING WAS STILL RAINY, AND when Hugh found Harry in the library as usual, he saw that the clouds had again gathered over the boy's spirit. He was pacing about the room in a very odd manner. The carpet was divided by colors in a regular pattern of diamonds. Harry's steps were, for the most part, planted on every third diamond as he slowly crossed the floor in a variety of directions. But every now and then the boy would make the most sudden and irregular change in his progression, setting his foot on the most unexpected diamond, at one time nearest to him, at another the farthest in his reach. When he looked up and saw his tutor watching him, still retaining the perplexed expression Hugh had noticed, Harry said, "How can God know on which of these diamonds I am going to set my foot next?"

"If you could understand how God knows, Harry, then you would know yourself. But before you have made up your mind, you don't know which you will choose, and even then you only know on which you intend to set your foot, for you have often changed your mind after making it up."

Harry looked as puzzled as before.

"Why, Harry, to understand how God understands, you would need to be as wise as he is. So it is no use trying. You see, you can't quite understand me, though I have a real meaning in what I say."

"I see it is no use. But I can't bear to be puzzled."

80

"But you need not be puzzled. You have no business to be puzzled. You are trying to get into your little brain what is far too grand and beautiful to get into it. Would you not think it very stupid to puzzle yourself how to put a hundred horses into a stable with twelve stalls?"

Harry laughed and looked relieved.

"It is a thousand times more unreasonable to try to understand such things. It would make me miserable to think that there was nothing but what I could understand."

The Tutor's First Love, pp. 61–62

And the peace of God, which passeth all
understanding, shall keep your hearts and
minds through Christ Jesus.
Philippians 4:7

God forbid that I should seem to despise understanding. The New Testament is full of urgings to understand. What I cry out upon is the misunderstanding that comes of man's endeavor to understand while not obeying.

Upon obedience must our energy be spent; understanding will follow. Not anxious to know our duty, or knowing it and not doing it, how shall we understand that which only a true heart and a clean soul can ever understand? The power in us that would understand if it were free lies in the bonds of imperfection and impurity and is therefore incapable of judging the divine. It cannot see the truth. If it could see it, it would not know it, and would not have it. *Knowing the Heart of God, p. 214;*
The Hope of the Gospel—"Salvation From Sin"

THE BONNY MAN

IN CONDITIONS OF CONSCIOUSNESS known only to himself, the poor fellow sustained an all but continuous hand-to-hand struggle with insanity, more or less agonized according to the nature and force of its vying assault; in which struggle, if not always victorious, he had yet never been defeated. Often tempted to escape misery by death, he had hitherto stood firm. Some part of every solitary night was spent, I imagine, in fighting that other evil suggestion. Doubtless what kept him lord of himself through all the truth-aping delusions that used his consciousness was his unyielding faith in the bonny man.

The name by which he so constantly thought and spoke of as the savior of men was not of his own finding. The story was well known of the idiot who, having partaken of the Lord's Supper, was heard murmuring to himself as he retired, "Oh, the bonny man! the bonny man!" And there were many persons, sound in mind as large of heart, who thought the idiot might well have seen him who came to deliver them that were bound. Steenie took up the tale with a most believing mind. Never doubting the man had seen the Lord, he responded with the passionate desire himself to see the *bonny man*. It awoke in him while yet quite a boy, and never left him, but increased as he grew, and became a fixed idea, a sober waiting, an unebbing passion, urging him to righteousness and lovingkindness. *The Peasant Girl's Dream, pp. 88–89*

O continue thy lovingkindness unto them
that know thee; and thy righteousness
to the upright in heart.
Psalm 36:10

THE ONE PRAYER—
DESIRING GOD'S WILL

"WHAT DO YOU PRAY FOR, THEN?"

"I have never yet required to ask anything not included in the prayer, 'Thy will be done!'"

"That will be done without your praying for it."

"Perhaps if you view those words of Christ's as a vague general prayer that somehow or other God's will in the universe will be done, I suppose you are right. But that prayer is far more personal than most people realize. And thus I do *not* believe it will be done, to all eternity, in the place where it needs doing the most, without my praying for it."

"Where is that?"

"Is it not in myself in my own heart? And how is his will to be done in me without my willing it? Does he not want me to love what he loves? To be like himself? To do his will with the glad effort of my will? In a word, to will what he wills? And when I find I cannot, what am I to do but pray for help? I pray, and he helps me."

"There is nothing so strange in that!"

"Surely not. It seems to me the simplest of common sense. It is my business, the business of every man, every woman, every child, that God's will be done by their obedience to that will the moment they know it."

The Landlady's Master, p. 142

Our Father which art in heaven, Hallowed be thy name. Thy kingdom come. Thy will be done, as in heaven, so in earth.
Luke 11:2

CHILDHOOD
THOUGHTLESSNESS
OVER THE FUTURE

THERE REMAINED FOR THE CHILD JUST A YEAR more of the farm, with all the varieties of life which had been so dear to her. Auntie Meg made sure she prepared her for the coming change. But it seemed to Annie so long in coming that it never would arrive. While the year lasted she gave herself up to the childish pleasures of the place without thinking of their approaching separation.

And why should Annie think of the future when the present was full of such delights? If she did not receive much tenderness from Auntie, at least she was not afraid of her. The pungency of her temper acted as salt and vinegar to bring out the true flavor of the other number-less pleasures around her. Were her excursions far afield, perched aloft on Dowie's shoulder, any less delightful because Auntie was scolding at home? And if she was late for one of her meals and Auntie declared she should have to fast, there still remained rosy-faced Emma who connived to surreptitiously bring the child the best of everything that was at hand, and put cream in her milk and butter on her oatcake. And Brownie was always friendly; ever ready for a serious emergency, when Auntie's temper was less than placid, to yield a corner of her stall as a refuge for the child. And the cocks and hens, and even the peacock and turkey, knew her perfectly and would come when she called them—if not altogether out of affection for her, at least out of hope in her bounty. And she would ride the horses to water, sitting sideways on their broad backs like a barefooted lady.

And then there were the great delights of the harvest field. With the reapers she would remain from morning till night, sharing in their meals and lightening their labor with her gentle frolic. Every day after the noon meal she would go to sleep on the shady side of a stook of straw, on two or three sheaves which Dowie would lay down for her in a choice spot.

Indeed, the little mistress was very fond of sleep and would go to sleep anywhere; this habit being indeed one of her aunt's chief grounds of complaint. Before haytime, for instance, when the grass in the fields was long, if she came upon any place that took her fancy she would tumble down at once and fall asleep on it. On such occasions it was no easy task to find her in the midst of the long grass that closed over her. But in the harvest field, at least, no harm could come of this habit, for *Dooie*, as she always called him, watched over her like a mother.

The only discomfort of the harvest field was that the sharp stubble forced her to wear shoes. But when the grain had all been carted home and the potatoes had been dug up and heaped in warm pits for the winter, and the mornings and evenings grew cold, then she had to put on both shoes and socks, which she did not like at all.

So through a whole winter of ice and snow, through a whole spring of promises slowly fulfilled, through a summer of glory, and another autumn of harvest joy, the day drew nearer when they must leave the farm. And still to Annie it seemed as far off as ever.

The Maiden's Bequest, pp. 22–23

And if ye lend to them of whom ye hope to receive, what thank have ye? for sinners also lend to sinners, to receive as much again.
Luke 6:34

GOD DOES NOT ALWAYS GIVE US OUR RIGHTS

"BUT, DONALD, NONE OF YOU WILL DIE of cold, and I can't let you fight, because the wives and children would then all be on my hands, and I would have more than my meal could feed. No, we must not fight. We may have a right to fight, I do not know. But I *am* sure we have the right to abstain from fighting. I don't let us confuse right and duty, Donald."

"Will the law not help us, Macruadh?"

"The law is a slow coach! Our enemies are rich, and the lawyers have little love of righteousness! Most of them would see the dust on our heads to have the picking of our bones. No stick or stone would be left us before anything came of a legal recourse."

"But, sir," said Donald, "is it the part of brave men to give up their rights?"

"No man can take our rights from us," answered the chief, "but any rich man may keep us from getting the good of them. Again I say, we are not bound to insist on our rights. If we decline to do so, that may give God the opportunity to look after us all the better."

The Highlander's Last Song, pp. 241–242

Judge me, O God, and plead my cause
against an ungodly nation: O deliver me
from the deceitful and unjust man.
Psalm 43:1

WOULD ANOTHER MINUTE MAKE A DIFFERENCE?

"YOU KNOW SOMETHING OF MY HISTORY: what would you have me do now, at once I mean What would the Person you are speaking of have me do?"

"That is not for me to say, my lord."

"You could give me a hint."

"No. God himself is telling you. For me to presume to tell you would be to interfere with him. What he would have a man do he lets him know in his mind."

"But what if I had not made up my mind before the last came?"

"Then I fear he would say to you, 'Depart from me, you worker of iniquity.'"

"That would be hard when another minute might have done it."

"If another minute would have done it, you would have had it." *The Fisherman's Lady, p. 263*

Behold, now is the accepted time; behold,
now is the day of salvation.
2 Corinthians 6:2

THE PATH TO GOD COMES THROUGH OUR FELLOWS

THE AUTUMN BROUGHT TERRIBLE STORMS. Many fishing boats came to grief. Of some, the crews lost everything: of others, the loss of their lives delivered them from the smaller losses. There were many bereaved families in the village, and Donal went about amongst them, doing what he could and seeking help for them where his own ability would not reach their necessity. Lady Arctura needed no persuasion to go with him on many of his visits, and this interchange with humanity in its simpler forms was of the greatest service in her renewed efforts to lay hold upon the skirt of the Father of men. She did not yet know that to love our neighbor is to be religious; and the man who does so will soon find that he cannot do without that higher part of religion, which is the love of God, without which the rest will sooner or later die away. She found the path to God the easier that she was now walking it in company with her fellows. We do not understand the next page of God's lesson book; we see only the one before us. Nor shall we be allowed to turn the leaf until we have learned its lesson. *The Shepherd's Castle, p. 169*

Love worketh no ill to his neighbour: therefore
love is the fulfilling of the law.
Romans 13:10

BE LIKE GOD,
NOT LIKE OTHERS

"GOD IS NEARER TO YOU THAN ANY thought or feeling of yours, Lady Emily. Do not be afraid. If all the evil things in the universe were around us, they could not come inside the ring that he makes about us. He always keeps a place for himself and his child into which no other being can enter."

"Oh, how you must love God, Margaret. You always speak of him as though he were your closest friend."

"Indeed I do love him, my lady. And that is just what he is. If ever anything looks beautiful or lovely to me, then I know at once that God is in it."

"Oh, you are a comfort to me, Margaret," Lady Emily said after a short silence. "Where did you learn such things?"

"From my father, and from God himself showing them to me in my heart."

"Ah, that is why I often feel when you come into my room as if the sun were shining and the wind were blowing in the treetops and the birds were singing. You seem to make everything clear, and right and plain. I wish I were you, Margaret."

"But how much better, my lady, to be what God chooses to make of you. To be made by God, is that not the grandest, most precious thing in all the world?"

The Tutor's First Love, p. 121

As Christ was raised up from the dead by the glory of the Father, even so we also should walk in newness of life.

Romans 6:4

Applying the Truth in the Workplace

"THAT'S THE BEAUTY OF IT!—EXCUSE ME, sir," cried the draper triumphantly. "You don't pretend to teach us anything, but you make us so uncomfortable that we go about afterward asking ourselves what we ought to do. Till last Sunday I had always considered myself a perfectly honest man. Let me see, it would be more correct to say I looked on myself as *quite honest enough*. I feel differently now, and that is your doing. You said in your sermon last Sunday, and especially to businessmen, 'Do you do to your neighbor as you would have your neighbor do to you? If not, how can you suppose that the Lord will acknowledge you as a disciple of his, that is, as a Christian?' Now, I was even surer of being a Christian than of being an honest man. I had satisfied myself more or less, that I had gone through all the necessary stages of being born again, and it has now been many years since I was received into a Christian church. At first, I was indignant at being called to question from a church pulpit whether or not I was a Christian. But I was driven from the theologians' tests who reduce the question to one of formulas and so-called belief. You sent me to try myself by the words of the Master instead—for he must be the best theologian of all, mustn't he? And so there and then I tried the test of doing to your neighbor as you would be done by. But I could not get it to work. I could not quite see how to apply it, and in thinking about it, I lost all the rest of the sermon.

"Now, whether it was anything you said coming back to me I cannot tell, but the next day—that was yesterday—all at once in the shop here, as I was serving

Mrs. Ramshorn, the thought came to me, *What would Jesus Christ have done if he had been a draper instead of a carpenter?* When she was gone, I went up to my room to think about it. First I determined I must know how he behaved as a carpenter. But we are told nothing about that. And so my thoughts turned again to the original question, *What would he have done had he been a draper?* And strange to say, I seemed to know far more about that than the other. In fact, I had a sharp and decisive answer concerning several things soon after I asked myself that question. And the more I thought, the more dissatisfied I became. That same afternoon, after hearing one of my clerks trying to persuade an old farmer's wife to buy some fabric pieces she didn't need, I called all my people together and told them that if I ever heard one of them doing such a thing in the future, I would turn him or her away at once. But unfortunately, I had some time before introduced the system of a small percentage to my clerks in order to induce them to do that very thing. I shall be able to rectify that at once, however. But I do wish I had something more definite to follow than merely doing as I would have others do to me."

"Would not more light inside do as well as clearer law outside?" suggested Wingfold.

The Curate's Awakening, pp. 100–101

Therefore all things whatsoever ye would that men should do to you, do ye even so to them: for this is the law and the prophets.
Matthew 7:12

TRUE KNOWING

"I HAVE HEARD MR. WINGFOLD SAY," continued Dorothy, "that however men may have been driven to form their ideas of God before Christ came, no man can, with thorough honesty, take the name of Christian whose ideas of the Father of men are gathered from any other field than the life, thought, words, and deeds of the only Son of that Father. He says it is not from the Bible as a book that we are to draw our ideas of God, but from the living Man into whose presence that book brings us, who is alive now, and gives his Spirit that they who read about him may understand what kind of being he is."

"I suspect," returned the minister, "that I have been far off the mark. But after this we will seek our Father together, in his Son, Jesus Christ."

This talk proved to be the initiation of a daily lesson together in the New Testament. While it drew their hearts to each other, it drew them gradually nearer and nearer to the ideal of humanity, Jesus Christ, in whom is the fullness of the Father.

A man may look another in the face for a hundred years and not know him. Men *have* looked Jesus Christ in the face, and not known either him or his Father. It was necessary that he should appear, to begin the knowing of him, but his visible presence was quickly taken away so that it would not become a veil to hide from the Father of their spirits. Many long for some sensible sign or intellectual proof. But such would only delay and impair that better, that best, vision—a contact with the heart of God himself, a perception of his being imparted by his spirit. For the sake of the vision God longs to give you, you are denied the vision you want. The Father of

our spirits is not content that we should know him as we now know each other. There is a better, closer, and nearer way than any human way of knowing, and he is guiding us to that across all the swamps of our unteachableness, the seas of our faithlessness, the deserts of our ignorance.

Is it so very hard to wait for that which we cannot yet receive? Shall we complain of the shadows cast upon the mirrors of our souls by the hand and the polishing cloth, to receive more excellent glory? Have patience, children of the Father. Pray always, and do not faint. The mists and the storms and the cold will pass: the sun and the sky are forever. The most loving of you cannot imagine how one day the love of the Father will make you love. Even your own. *The Lady's Confession, p. 150*

Lead me in thy truth, and teach me: for thou art the God of my salvation; on thee do I wait all the day.
Psalm 25:5

Faster and faster will the glory of the Lord dawn upon the hearts and minds of his people walking in obedience. Then they are his people indeed! Fast and far will the knowledge of him spread, for truth of action, both preceding and following truth of word, will prepare the way before him.

The man and woman walking in the truth they know will be able to think aright. Only when we begin to do the thing we know do we begin to think aright. Then God comes to us in a new and higher way. *Knowing the Heart of God, p. 47;*

Unspoken Sermons, Second Series—"The Truth in Jesus"

PROOF IS NOT BELIEF

"THEN WHY DO YOU BELIEVE IT?" ASKED Barbara.

"Belief and proof have little or nothing to do with each other. I believe many things I cannot prove. I believe in God, but I could never begin to prove his existence to one who wanted to argue the point."

"But," persisted Barbara, with Richard in her mind, "how are you to be sure of what you can't prove?"

"When you love a thing, you already believe enough to put it to the proof of trial rather than the proof of brains. Shall I search heaven and earth for proof that my wife is a good and lovely woman? The signs of it are everywhere; the proofs of it nowhere."

The Baron's Apprenticeship, p. 114

The heavens declare the glory of God; and the firmament sheweth his handywork.
Psalm 19:1

The heavens declare his righteousness, and all the people see his glory.
Psalm 97:6

IT IS MORE LIFE WE WANT

THE SUMMER CAME AGAIN, AND THEN THE harvest, and with it once more the opportunity for Cosmo to earn a pound or two. But he determined this time not to go so far from home to find work, for he could see that his father's spirits and energy were better the more he was with him. Left alone, he began at once to go home the faster—as if another dragging anchor were cast loose, and he was drawn the more swiftly where the tides of life originate. To the old and weary man the life to come appeared as rest; to the young and active Cosmo it promised more work.

But it is all the same—what we need for rest as well as for labor is *life*; it is more life we want, and that is everything. The eternal root causes us to long for more existence, more being, more of God's making, less of our own unmaking.   *The Laird's Inheritance, p. 254*

Come unto me, all ye that labour and are
heavy laden, and I will give you rest.
Matthew 11:28

Let us labour therefore to enter into that rest,
lest any man fall after the same example
of unbelief.
Hebrews 4:11

Interest in God Is Not a Relationship With Him

He had been much more of a religious man than the major, but it was the *idea* of religion, and the thousand ideas it broods, more than the practice of it daily, that was his delight. He philosophized and philosophized well of the relations between man and his maker, of the necessity to human nature of a belief in a God, of the disastrous consequences of having none, and suchlike things. But having an interest in God is a very different thing from living in such a close relationship with the Father that the thought of him is an immediate and ever-returning joy and strength. He was so busy understanding with his intellect that he missed the better understanding of heart and imagination. He was always so pleased with the thought of a thing that he missed the thing itself—whose *possession*, not its thought, is essential. Love is at the heart of every right way, and essential forgiveness at the heart of every true treatment of the sinner.   *The Gentlewoman's Choice, p. 186*

Then cried Jesus in the temple as he taught,
saying, Ye both know me, and ye know
whence I am: and I am not come of myself,
but he that sent me is true,
whom ye know not.
John 7:28

HE WHO OBEYS, SHINES

THERE WAS A SECRET BETWEEN THEM—A secret proclaimed on the housetops, a secret hidden, the most precious of pearls, in their hearts—that the earth is the Lord's and the fullness thereof. Before everyman's eyes this secret silently shouts its truth, yet remains unseen and unheard by all but those with eyes to see and ears to hear. A secret it was indeed, yet the most life-giving truth in all the world—that the work done on the earth is the work of the Lord, whether the sowing of the field, the milking of the cow, the giving to the poor, the spending of wages, the reading of the Bible; that God is all in all, and every throb of gladness is his gift; that their life came fresh every moment from his heart, that what was lacking to them would arrive the very moment he had got them ready for it.

They were God's little ones in God's world. Among the poverty-stricken Christians, consumed with care to keep a hold of the world and save their souls, they were as two children of the house. By living in the presence of the living one, they had themselves become his presence—dim lanterns through which his light shone steady.

He who obeys, shines.   *The Landlady's Master, pp. 80–81*

The earth is the Lord's, and the fulness thereof;
the world, and they that dwell therein. For he
hath founded it upon the seas, and established
it upon the floods.
Psalm 24:1–2

A CHRISTIAN'S RESPONSIBILITY

"THERE ARE A THOUSAND PROMISES MADE every day which nobody is expected to keep. It is the custom, the way of the world. How many of the clergy believe the things they say?"

"They must answer for themselves. We are not clergymen, but women, who ought never to say a thing except we mean it, and when we have said it, to stick to it."

"But just look around you and see how many there are in precisely the same position as me. Will you dare to say they are all going to be lost because they do not behave like angels to their brutes of husbands?"

"I say they have got to repent of behaving to their husbands as their husbands behave to them. What someone else does has nothing to do with it. The responsibility of a Christian is clear no matter that everyone else goes their own selfish way."

"And what if they don't repent?"

Mary paused a little.

"Do you expect to go to heaven, ma'am?" she asked.

"I hope so."

"Do you think you will like it?"

"I must say, I think it will be rather dull."

"Then, to use your own word, you must be very like lost anyway. There does not seem to be a right place for you anywhere, and that is very like being lost, is it not?"

Hesper laughed.

"I am pretty comfortable where I am," she said.

Husband and all! thought Mary, but she did not say that. What she said was: "But you know you can't stay

here. God is not going to keep up this way of things for you. And how can you expect it when you don't care a straw what he wants of you? I have sometimes thought— What if hell were just a place where God gives everybody everything they want, and lets everybody do whatever they like, without once coming to interfere! What a hell that would be! For God's presence in the very being, and nothing else, is bliss. That, then, would be the very opposite of heaven, and very much the opposite of this world. Such a hell would go on, I suppose, till every one had learned to hate everyone else in the world."   *A Daughter's Devotion, pp. 212–213*

Give to every man that asketh of thee; and of him that taketh away thy goods ask them not again. And as ye would that men should do to you, do ye also to them likewise. For if ye love them which love you, what thank have ye? for sinners also love those that love them. And if ye do good to them which do good to you, what thank have ye? for sinners also do even the same. And if ye lend to them of whom ye hope to receive, what thank have ye? for sinners also lend to sinners, to receive as much again. But love ye your enemies, and do good, and lend, hoping for nothing again; and your reward shall be great, and ye shall be the children of the Highest: for he is kind unto the unthankful and to the evil. Be ye therefore merciful, as your Father also is merciful.
Luke 6:30–36

SOME PRETEND TO BE WHILE OTHERS ARE

"REALLY, MR. SCLATER," HIS WIFE CONTINUED, "I had no idea what I was undertaking. But you gave me no choice. The creature is incorrigible. But of course he must prefer the society of women like that. They are the sort he was accustomed to when he received his first impressions, and how could it be otherwise? You knew how he had been brought up, and what you had to expect!"

"Brought up," cried the minister. "You should have seen him about the streets!"

Nothing further was said until the second course was on the table. Then the lady spoke again.

"You really must teach him the absurdity of attempting to fit every point of his behavior to—to—words which were of course quite suitable to the time when they were spoken, but which it is impossible to take literally nowadays. Why! You saw him throw his arms around the horrid creature's neck! Well, he had just asked me if she was a sinner. I made no doubt she was. With the word, off goes my gentleman to embrace her!"

Here they laughed together.

Dinner over, they went to a missionary meeting, where the one stood and made a speech and the other sat and listened, while Gibbie was having tea with Mistress Croale. *The Baronet's Song, pp. 157–158*

An hypocrite with his mouth destroyeth his neighbour: but through knowledge shall the just be delivered.
Proverbs 11:9

POLWARTH'S PRAYER

"'Strength is made perfect in weakness.' Hearing a grand principle such as that spoken in its widest application, as a fact not just of humanity but of all creation, brings me close to the very heart of the universe. Strength itself—of all kinds—is made perfect in weakness. This is not just a law of Christian growth, but a law of growth itself. Even the Master's strength was thus perfected."

Polwarth slipped from his stool and knelt beside the table; Rachel did likewise.

"O Father of life," he prayed, "we praise you that you will one day take your poor crooked creatures and give them bodies like Christ's, perfect and full of light. Help us to grow faster—as fast as you can help us grow. Help us to keep our eyes on the opening of your hand, that we may know the manna when it comes. We rejoice that we are your making, though your handiwork is not very plain yet in the outer man. We bless you that we feel your hand making us, even if what we feel be pain. Always we hear the voice of the potter above the hum and grind of the wheel. Fashion the clay to your will. You have made us love you and hope in you, and in your love we will be brave and endure. All in good time, O Lord. Amen." *The Lady's Confession, pp. 202–203*

And he said unto me, My grace is sufficient for thee: for my strength is made perfect in weakness. Most gladly therefore will I rather glory in my infirmities, that the power of Christ may rest upon me.
2 Corinthians 12:9

A FATHER'S PRAYER FOR A PRODIGAL SON

"IT'S AWFUL TO THINK—I HARDLY DARE SAY it, Peter! But was no minister o' the gospel ever a heepocreete?—like one o' the auld scribes an' Pharisees? Oh, Peter, wouldna it be terrible if oor only ain son was—"

But here she broke down and could not finish the frightful sentence. The farmer left his bed and dropped into a chair beside it. The next moment he sank on his knees, and hiding his face in his hand, groaned, as from a thicket of torture.

"God in heaven, hae mercy upon the whole lot o' us!"

Then, apparently unconscious of what he did, he went wandering from the room, down the kitchen, and out to the barn on his bare feet, closing the door of the house behind him. In the barn he threw himself face downward on a heap of loose straw and lay there motionless. His wife wept alone in her bed, and hardly missed him. It required little reflection on her part to understand where he had gone or what he was doing. He was crying from the bitterness of a wounded father's heart, to the Father of fathers.

"God, ye're a father, yerself," he groaned, "an sae ye ken hoo it's tearin' at my heart! I'm no accusin' Jimmie, lad, for ye ken weel hoo little I ken aboot him. He never opened the book o' his heart to me! Oh, God, grant that he has nothin' to hide; but if he has, Lord, pluck it oot o' him, an' him oot o' the mud. I dinna ken hoo to pray for him, Lord, for I'm in the dark. But deliver him some way, Lord, I pray thee, for his mither's sake. Lord, deliver

the heart o' her frae the awfulest o' all her fears at her ain son's a hypocreet, a Judas-man!"

He remained there praying upon the straw while hour after hour passed, pleading with the great Father for his son; his soul now lost in dull fatigue, until at length the dawn looked in on the night-weary earth, and into the two sorrow-laden hearts, bringing with it a comfort they did not seek to understand.

The Minister's Restoration, pp 100–101

He that wasteth his father, and chaseth away
his mother, is a son that causeth shame, and
bringeth reproach.
Proverbs 19:26

Come, sore heart, and see whether Christ's heart can heal yours. He knows what sighs and tears are, and if he knew no sin himself, the more pitiful must it have been to look on the sighs and tears that guilt wrung from the tortured hearts of his brothers and sisters. Beloved, we *must* get rid of this misery of ours. It is slaying us. It is turning the fair earth into a hell, and our hearts into its fuel.

There stands the Man who says he knows; take him at his word. Go to him who says in the power of his eternal tenderness and his pity, "Come unto me, all ye that labor and are heavy laden, and I will give you rest. Take my yoke upon you, and learn of me; for I am meek and lowly in heart: and you shall find rest for your souls. For my yoke is easy, and my burden is light!

Discovering the Character of God, p. 195;
The Curate's Awakening, p. 115

I HAVE THE RIGHT TO YIELD MY RIGHT

HERE WAS THE OPPORTUNITY OF WHICH
Ian had spoken.

"This may be just the sort of thing Jesus meant!" he
said aloud. "Even if I be in the right, I have a right to
yield my right—and to *him* I will yield it."

No sooner had he yielded his pride and begun to feel
the joy of deliverance from self rushing into his heart than
a pity began to awake inside him for Sercombe. Might it
be possible to love the man—not for anything he was but
for what he might and must someday be in God?

Yet even with the thought again and again swelled the
tide of wrath and unwillingness, making him feel as if he
could not carry out his resolve. But all the time he knew
the thing was as good as done—it had already been determined and nothing could now turn it aside.

The Highlander's Last Song, pp. 138–139

*A man's pride shall bring him low: but
honour shall uphold the humble in spirit.*
Proverbs 29:23

It is a very small matter to you whether another
man does *you* right. It is life or death to you whether
you do *him* right. If, owing you love, he gives you
hate, you, owing him love, have yet to pay it.

Discovering the Character of God, p. 293;
Unspoken Sermons, Second Series—"The Last Farthing"

THE LEVELING OF DISTINCTIONS

AS THE DAYS WENT BY, COSMO'S ENGAGE-
ment to Mr. Henderson drew near. No doubt the farmer
would have let him out of it at once, but not for a moment
did Cosmo consider trying to back out of it because he
was now in plenty. He would never have considered a
thing disgraceful only because he was a rich man. No
true man will ever ask of a fellow creature, man or
woman, the doing of a thing he himself would feel
degraded to do. There is nothing like Christianity to
make all men equal, to level such distinctions—but it
levels by lifting to a lofty tableland, accessible only to
humility. Only he who is humble can rise.

So Cosmo's thought was not to gain respect by thus
holding to what he had undertaken, but simply to hon-
orably and gratefully fulfill his contract. Not only would
it have been a poor return for Mr. Henderson's kindness
to treat his service as something beneath him now, but,
worst of all, it would have been to accept ennoblement
at the hands of Mammon, as of a power able to alter his
station in God's world. To change the spirit of one's way
because of money is to confess oneself a born slave, a
thing only with an outside and no heart, a Knight of
Riches with a maggot for his crest.

The Laird's Inheritance, p. 340

*The fear of the Lord is the instruction of
wisdom; and before honour is humility.*
Proverbs 15:33

Respect for God or for Religion?

"Is she a sinner?" he asked.

Mrs. Sclater nodded.

Gibbie wheeled round and sprang back to the hall, whither the minister had ejected Mistress Croale and was now talking to her with an air of confidential condescension, willing to wipe out any feeling of injury she might perhaps be inclined to cherish at not being made more welcome. To the minister's consternation, Gibbie threw his arms round her neck and gave her a great hug.

"Sir Gilbert!" he exclaimed, the more angry that he knew Gibbie was in the right, "leave Mistress Croale alone, and go back to your dinner immediately. Jane, open the door."

Jane opened the door, Gibbie let her go, and Mrs. Croale went. But on the threshold she turned to the minister: "Well, sir," she said, with a certain sad injury not unmingled with dignity, "you have stepped over my doorstep many times, and with sorer words in your mouth than I used to pay you back. And I never told you to go. So first you turn me out of my own house and now you turn me out of yours; and what's left for you but to turn me out of the house of the Lord? And, indeed, sir, you need never wonder if the likes of me doesn't care about coming to hear the preached gospel—we would fain see a practiced one!"

"You shall have a plate of soup, and welcome, Mistress Croale" said the minister. "Jane, take Mistress Croale to the kitchen with you, and—"

"The devil's tail in your soup!" cried Mistress Croale, drawing herself up suddenly. "When did I turn into a

beggar? Was it your soup or your grace I sought for, sir? The Lord judge between me and you! There's first that will be last, and last that will be first. But the one's not me, and the other's not you, sir."

With this she turned and walked down the steps, holding her head high.

"Really, Sir Gilbert," said the minister, going back into the dining room—but no Gibbie was there! Nobody but his wife, sitting in solitary discomposure at the head of the dinner table. The same instant he heard a clatter of feet down the steps and turned quickly into the hall again, where Jane was in the act of shutting the door.

"Sir Gilbert's run out after the woman, sir!" she said.

"Hoot!" grunted the minister, greatly displeased, and went back to his wife.

"Take Sir Gilbert's plate away," said Mrs. Sclater to the servant.

"That's his New Testament again!" she went on, when the girl had left the room.

"My dear! my dear! take care," said her husband. He had not much notion of obedience to God, but he had some idea of respect to religion.

The Baronet's Song, pp. 156–157

If any man among you seem to be religious, and bridleth not his tongue, but deceiveth his own heart, this man's religion is vain. Pure religion and undefiled before God and the Father is this, To visit the fatherless and widows in their affliction, and to keep himself unspotted from the world.
James 1:26–27

SHARE THE HARVEST

IN DUE TIME HARVEST CAME; AND ANNIE could no more keep from haunting the harvest than the crane could keep from flying south when the summer was over. She watched all the fields around Glamerton; she knew what response each made to the sun and which would first be ripe for reaping. And the very day that the sickle was put in, there was Annie to see and share in the joy. Unquestioned as uninvited, she became one of the company of reapers, gatherers, binders, and stookers, assembled to collect the living gold of the earth from the early fields of the farm of Howglen.

The laborers all knew her well and themselves took care that she should have the portion of their food which her assistance had well earned. She never refused anything that was offered her except money. That she had taken only once in her life—from Mr. Cowie, whom she continued to love the more dearly, although she no longer attended his church.

But again the harvest was safely lodged and the sad old age of the year sank through the rains and forests to his grave. *The Maiden's Bequest, pp. 137–138*

*And thou shalt not glean thy vineyard,
neither shalt thou gather every grape of thy
vineyard; thou shalt leave them for the poor
and stranger: I am the Lord your God.
Leviticus 19:10*

TAKING DARK FOR LIGHT

"DON'T YOU THINK YOU ARE GOING JUST A little too far there, Mr. Maclear?" the parson said.

"Ye mean too far into the dark, Mr. Blatherwick?"

"Yes. You speculate too boldly where there is no light to show what might be and what might not."

"But dinna ye think, sir, that that's the very direction where the dark grows a wee bit thinner, though I grant ye there's nothing yet to call light?"

"But the human soul is just as apt to deceive itself as the human eye. It is always ready to take a flash inside itself for something real," said Blatherwick.

"Nae doobt, nae doobt! But when the true light comes, ye aye ken the difference! A man *may* take the dark for light, but he canna take the light for darkness!"

"And there must always be something for the light to shine upon, otherwise the man sees nothing," said the parson.

"Maybe, like the Ephesians, ye haena yet found oot aboot the Holy Spirit, sir?"

"No man dares deny that!"

"But a man might not *know* it, though he dares not deny it. None but them that follows where he leads can ken truthfully that he is."   *The Minister's Restoration, p 62*

I the Lord have called thee in righteousness,
and will hold thine hand, and will keep thee,
and give thee for a covenant of the people, for
a light of the Gentiles.
Isaiah 42:6

Would Any Kind of God Meet Your Requirements?

"The question is not of the idea of a God, but of the existence of God. And if he exists, he must be such as the human heart could never accept as God because of the cruelty he permits."

"I grant that argument a certain amount of force, and that very thing has troubled me at times, but I am coming to see it in a different light. I heard some children the other day saying that Dr. Faber was a very cruel man, for he pulled out nurse's tooth, and gave poor little baby such a nasty, nasty powder."

"Is that a fair parallel?" asked Faber.

"I think it is. What you do is often unpleasant, sometimes most painful, but it does not follow that you are a cruel man, one that hurts rather than heals."

"I think there is fault in the analogy," objected Faber. "I am nothing but a slave to laws already existing, and compelled to work according to them. It is not my fault, therefore, that the remedies I have to use are unpleasant. But if there be a God, he has the matter in his own hands."

"But suppose," suggested the curate, "that the design of God involved the perfecting of men as the children of God. Suppose his grand idea could not be content with creatures perfect only by his gift but also involved in partaking of God's individuality and free will and choice of good. And suppose that suffering were the only way through which the individual soul could be set, in separate and self-individuality, so far apart from God that it might *will* and so become a partaker of his single-

ness and freedom. And suppose that God saw the seed of a pure affection, say in your friend and his wife, but saw also that it was a seed so imperfect and weak that it could not encounter the coming frosts and winds of the world without loss and decay. Yet, if they were parted now for a few years, it would grow and strengthen and expand to the certainty of an infinitely higher and deeper and keener love through the endless ages to follow—so that by suffering should come, in place of contented decline, abortion, and death, a troubled birth of joyous result in health and immortality—suppose all this, what then?"

Faber was silent a moment, and then answered, "Your theory has but one fault; it is too good to be true."

"My theory leaves plenty of difficulty, but has no such fault as that. Why, what sort of a God would content you, Mr. Faber? The one idea is too bad to be true, the other too good. Must you expand and trim until you get one exactly to the measure of yourself before you can accept it as thinkable or possible? Why, a God like that would not test your soul a week. The only possibility of believing in a God seems to me in finding an idea of God large enough, grand enough, pure enough, lovely enough to be fit to believe in."

The Curate's Awakening, pp. 172–173

Thus saith the Lord, The heaven is my throne, and the earth is my footstool: where is the house that ye build unto me? and where is the place of my rest?
Isaiah 66:1

LEARNING OF THE LIGHT

THEN GREW IN THE MIND OF THE MINISTER the realization that divine things can only be shadowed in the human. As the heavens are higher than the earth, so are God's ways higher than ours, and what we call his forgiveness may be, must be, something altogether transcending the understanding of man.

Then it came into the minister's mind how when the young man asked Jesus what commandments he must keep that he might inherit eternal life, Jesus did not say a word concerning his duty toward God. He spoke only of his duty toward man. Then it struck him that our Lord gave him no sketch or summary of a religious system—he only told him what he asked, the practical steps by which he might begin to climb toward eternal life. One thing he lacked—namely, God himself; but as to how God would meet him, Jesus says nothing, but himself meets him on those steps with the offer of God. He treats the secondary duties (service to man) as a stair to the first (love to God)—a stair which, probably by crumbling away in failure beneath his feet as he ascended, would plunge him to such a horror of frustration as would make him stretch forth his hands, like the sinking Peter, to the living God. Only in that final surrender could the life eternal stoop to rescue him.

The Lady's Confession, p. 222

For as the heavens are higher than the earth,
so are my ways higher than your ways, and
my thoughts than your thoughts.
Isaiah 55:9

GOD IS INSIDE, OUTSIDE— EVERYWHERE!

"EVEN IN THESE LOWLY THINGS, THERE IS A something that has its root deeper than your pain. All about us in earth and air, wherever eye or ear can reach, there is a power ever breathing itself forth in signs. Now it shows itself in a daisy, now in a waft of wind, a cloud, a sunset, and this power holds constant relation with the dark and silent world within us. The same God who is in us, and upon whose tree we are the buds, also is all about us—inside, the Spirit; outside, the Word. And the two are ever trying to meet in us; and when they meet, then the sign without and the longing within become one. The man no more walks in darkness, but in light, knowing where he is going." *The Curate's Awakening, p. 184*

Whither shall I go from thy spirit? or whither shall I flee from thy presence? If I ascend up into heaven, thou art there: if I make my bed in hell, behold, thou art there. If I take the wings of the morning, and dwell in the uttermost parts of the sea; even there shall thy hand lead me, and thy right hand shall hold me. If I say, Surely the darkness shall cover me; even the night shall be light about me. Yea, the darkness hideth not from thee; but the night shineth as the day: the darkness and the light are both alike to thee.

Psalm 139:7–12

PEACE COMES FROM DOING THE TRUTH

THE LABOR OF LOVE IS ITS OWN REWARD, but Dorothy received much more. For in the fresh impulse and freedom which resulted from this service, she soon found not only that she thought better and more clearly on the things that troubled her, but that, by giving herself, she grew more and more able to believe in one whose glory is perfect ministration. She was not finding an atom of what is called proof. But when the longing heart finds that the truth is alive, it can go on without such evidence that belongs to the lower stratum of things.

When we rise into the mountain air, we require no other testimony than our lungs that we are in a healthful atmosphere. We did not find it necessary to submit it to a quantitative analysis; we are content that we breathe with joy. Truth is a very different thing from fact; it is the loving contact of the soul with spiritual fact, vital and potent. It does its work in the soul independent of the soul's ability to explain it. Truth in the inward parts is a power, not an opinion.

How can it be otherwise? If God be so near as the very idea of him necessitates, what other proof of his existence can there be than such *awareness* as must come of the developing relation between him and us? The most satisfying of all intellectual proofs would be of no value. God would be no nearer us for them all. They would bring about no blossoming of the mighty fact.

Peace is for those who *do* the truth, not those who believe it intellectually. The true man troubled by doubts is so troubled into further health and growth. Let him be alive and hopeful, above all obedient, and he will be

able to wait for the deeper contentedness which must follow with more complete insight. Men such as Faber may say such as Wingfold deceive themselves. But this is at least worth reflecting on—that while the man who aspires to higher regions of life sometimes does fear he deceives himself, it is the man who aspires for nothing more whose eyes are not looking for truth from whatever quarter it pleases to come. The former has eyes open, the latter eyes closed. And so, as more and more truth is revealed, one day the former may be sure, and the latter begin to doubt in earnest!

The Lady's Confession, pp. 170–171

And ye shall seek me, and find me, when ye shall search for me with all your heart.
Jeremiah 29:13

Ambition in every form has to do with *things*, with outward advantages for the satisfaction of self-worship. It is that form of pride, foul shadow of Satan, that usurps the place of aspiration.

The sole ambition that is of God is the ambition to rise above oneself; all other is of the devil. Yet ambition is nursed and cherished in many a soul that thinks itself devout, filling it with petty cares and disappointments, that swarm like bats in its air, and shut out the glory of God.

The love of the praise of men, the desire for fame, the pride that takes offense, the puffing-up of knowledge, these and every other form of ever-changing self-worship—we must get rid of them all.

Knowing the Heart of God, p. 84;
Unspoken Sermons, Second Series—"The Cause of Spiritual Stupidity"

LOSS AWAKENS US TO A HIGHER NEED

FINDING THE CASTLE OF HER SELF, WHICH she had regarded as impregnable, now crumbling under the shot of the enemy, she found herself defenseless, and thus discovered refuge in her little maid, the daughter she had for so long ignored. The loss of all that the world counts *first things* is a thousand-fold repaid in the waking to higher need. It proves the presence of the divine in the lower good, that its loss is so potent. A man may send his gaze over the clear heaven and suspect no God. But when the stifling cloud comes down, folds itself about him, shuts from him the expanse of the universe, he begins to long for a hand, a sign, some shadow of presence. *The Baron's Apprenticeship, p. 146*

Hide not thy face from me in the day when I am in trouble; incline thine ear unto me: in the day when I call answer me speedily.
Psalm 102:2

Am I not a fool whenever loss troubles me more than recovery would gladden?

God would have me wise and smile at the trifle. Is it not time I lost a few things when I care for them so unreasonably? The losing of things is of the mercy of God; it comes to teach us to let them go. *Knowing the Heart of God, pp. 82–83;*
Unspoken Sermons, Second Series—"The Cause of Spiritual Stupidity"

WHEN WE ARE BROKEN, GOD'S SPIRIT CAN ENTER

MRS. WYLDER SOUGHT REFUGE IN LOVE; and what is the love of child, or mother, or dog, but the love of God shining through another being? The one important result of her illness, finding refuge in the love of her daughter, brought her to love Barbara. The next point in her eternal growth would be to love the God who made the child she loved, and whose love shone upon her through the child. By nature Mrs. Wylder was a strong woman whom passion made weak, hardening her will into selfish determination, then pulling it into helpless obstinacy. Where the temple of God has no windows, earthquakes must sometimes come to tear off the roof that sunlight may enter. Her earthquake had come, and Barbara's mother lay broken so that the spirit of her daughter might enter the soul of her mother—and with it the Spirit of him who, in the heart of her daughter, made her who she was. *The Baron's Apprenticeship, p. 146*

*I am like a broken vessel. For I have heard the
slander of many: fear was on every side:
while they took counsel together against me,
they devised to take away my life. But I
trusted in thee, O Lord: I said, Thou art my
God. My times are in thy hand: deliver me
from the hand of mine enemies, and from
them that persecute me.*
Psalm 31:12–16

WE KNOW GOD BY THE THINGS HE HAS MADE

"WHAT NOTION COULD WE HAVE HAD OF majesty if the heavens seemed scarcely higher than the earth? What feeling of the grandeur of God, of the vastness of his being, of the limitlessness of his goodness? For space is the body to our idea of God. Over and around us we have the one perfect geometrical shape—a dome, or a sphere. I do not say it is put there for the purpose of representing God. I say it is there of necessity, because of its nature in relation to God's nature and character. It is of God's thinking, and that half sphere above our heads is the beginning of all revelation of him to men. We must begin with that. It is the simplest as well as most external likeness of him, while its relation to him goes so deep that it represents things in his very nature that nothing else could."

"You bewilder me," said Mercy.

"Think how it would be if this blue sky was only a solid. Men in ancient times believed that; it is hardly a wonder their gods were so small. But no matter how high it was, if it was limited at all it could not declare the glory of God. But it is a sphere only to the eyes; it is a foreshortening of infinitude that it may enter our sight; there is no imagining its limit. This infinite sphere, then, is the only figure, image, or symbol fit to begin acquainting us with God; it is an idea incomprehensible, and we can only believe it. In like manner, God cannot be found out by searching, cannot be grasped by any mind, yet is ever before us, the one we can best know, the one we must

know, the one we cannot help but know. For his end in giving us being is that his humblest creature should at length know him utterly."

The Highlander's Last Song, pp. 152–153

When I consider thy heavens, the work of thy fingers, the moon and the stars, which thou hast ordained; What is man, that thou art mindful of him? and the son of man, that thou visitest him? For thou hast made him a little lower than the angels, and hast crowned him with glory and honour.

Psalm 8:3–5

All things are possible with God, but all things are not easy. It is easy for him *to be*, for there he has to do with his own perfect will. It is not easy for him to create. In the very nature of being, it must be hard—and divine history shows how hard—to create that which shall not be himself, yet like himself.

The problem is, so far to separate from himself that which must yet on him be ever and always and utterly dependent, that it shall have the existence of an individual, and be able to turn and regard him—choose him, and say, "I will arise and go to my Father," and so develop in itself the highest *divine* of which it is capable: the will for the good against the evil, the will to be one with the life whence it has come, the will to shape in its own life the ring of eternity, to be the thing the Maker thought of when he willed, before he began to work its being.

Discovering the Character of God, p. 87;
Unspoken Sermons, Second Series—"Life"

119

CRY TO HIM

"NOTHING BUT THE BURNING LOVE OF GOD can rid sin out of anywhere. But are you not forgetting him who surely knew what he undertook when he would save the world? You can no more tell what the love of God is, or what it can do for you, than you could have set that sun flaming overhead. Few men have such a cry to raise to the Father as you, such a claim of sin and helplessness to heave up before him. Cry to him, Leopold, my dear boy! Cry to him again and yet again, for he himself said that men ought always to pray and not to faint. God does hear and will answer although he might seem long about it."

The Curate's Awakening, pp. 184–185

And he spake a parable unto them to this end,
that men ought always to pray,
and not to faint.
Luke 18:1

The heart of God is the one and only goal of the human race.

There is no halfway house of rest, where ungodliness may be dallied with, and not prove quite fatal. Be they few or many cast into the prison of darkness, there can be no deliverance for a human soul, whether in that prison or out of it, but in paying the last farthing, in becoming lowly, penitent, self-refusing—so receiving the sonship, and learning to cry, "Father!"

Discovering the Character of God, p. 294;
Unspoken Sermons, Second Series—"The Last Farthing"

THE WILL OF GOD IS THE ROOT OF GLADNESS

RARELY WOULD WINGFOLD ENTER A sickroom, especially in a poor cottage, with a long face and a sermon in his soul. Almost always he walked lightly in, with a cheerful look and some kind of odd story on his tongue, well pleased when he could make the sufferer laugh—better pleased sometimes when he had made him sorry. He did not find those that laughed the readiest the hardest to make sorry. He moved his people by infecting their hearts with the feeling in his own.

Having now for many years cared only for the will of God, he was full of joy. For the will of the Father is the root of all his children's gladness, of all their laughter and merriment. The child that loves the will of the Father is at the heart of things; his will is with the motion of the eternal wheels; the eyes of all those wheels are opened upon him, and he knows whence he came. Happy and fearless and hopeful, he knows himself the child of him from whom he came, and his peace and joy break out in light. He rises and shines. No other bliss than the will of the Father, creative and energetic, exists on earth or in heaven. *The Baron's Apprenticeship, pp. 236–237*

A merry heart doeth good like a medicine: but
a broken spirit drieth the bones.
Proverbs 17:22

THE HEART MUST HAVE NO THINGS IN IT

TO BE LORD OF SPACE, A MAN MUST BE FREE of all bonds to place. To be heir of all things, his heart must have no *things* in it. He must be like him who makes things, not like one who would put everything in his pocket. He must stand on the upper, not the lower side of them, where he controls rather than is controlled. He must be as the man who makes poems, not the man who gathers books of verse. He must be as the man who absorbs the truths of a book and brings its principles into his daily life, not the man who collects books for their fine bindings. Only so do the *things*, the *poems*, the *books* become truly his eternal possession.

God, having made a sunset, lets it pass, and makes such a sunset never again. God has no picture-gallery, no library, no collections, no monuments to the past.

The Laird's Inheritance, pp. 300–301

*Lay not up for yourselves treasures upon
earth, where moth and rust doth corrupt, and
where thieves break through and steal: But
lay up for yourselves treasures in heaven,
where neither moth nor rust doth corrupt, and
where thieves do not break through nor steal:
For where your treasure is, there will
your heart be also.
Matthew 6:19–21*

WHICH GOD DO YOU DENY?

JOHN TUKE WAS A THINKING MAN—THAT IS, if a conversation was set in any direction that interested him, he could take a few steps forward without assistance. But he could start in no direction of himself. At a small club to which he belonged, he had come into contact with certain ideas new to him, and finding himself able to grasp them, felt at once as if they must be true. Certain other ideas, also new to him, which came self-suggested in their train, set him to imagining himself a thinker, able to generate notions beyond the grasp of people around him. He began to grow self-confident. He then took courage to deny things he had never believed, and finding that he gave offense, chose to imagine himself a martyr for the truth. He did not see that a denial involving no assertion cannot witness to any truth. Logically put, this rather flimsy position would have been: I never knew such things; I do not like the notion of them; therefore I deny them; they do not exist. But when John Tuke denied the God in his feeble notion, he denied only a God that could have no existence. *The Baron's Apprenticeship, p. 21*

Of these things put them in remembrance,
charging them before the Lord that they strive
not about words to no profit, but to the
subverting of the hearers.
2 Timothy 2:14

INSIDES AREN'T ALWAYS SO NICE-LOOKING AS OUTSIDES

ANNIE WANDERED AWAY UP THE FIELD toward a little old cottage. She knew that Thomas Crann was at work there and found him busy rough-casting the outside of it with plaster.

"You're busy working, Thomas," said Annie, for the sake of something to say.

"Ay, jist helpin' to make a hypocrite," answered Thomas, with a nod and a smile as he threw a trowelful of mortar against the wall.

"What do you mean by that?" asked Annie.

"If ye knew this old place as well as I do, ye wouldn't need to ask that question. It should have been pulled down from the riggin' to the foundation a century ago. An' here we're puttin' a clean face on it."

"It *looks* well enough."

"I told ye I was makin' a hypocrite," and he chuckled.

The Maiden's Bequest, p. 188

*Ye are like unto whited sepulchres, which
indeed appear beautiful outward, but are
within full of dead men's bones, and of all
uncleanness. Even so ye also outwardly
appear righteous unto men, but within ye are
full of hypocrisy and iniquity.*
Matthew 23:27–28

I WANT YOU TO BE JUST LIKE THE LORD JESUS

"MARY," HE SAID, "COME HERE. I WANT TO speak to you." She knelt down beside him.

"Mary," he said again, taking her hand in his two long, bony ones, "I love you, my child, more than I know how to say. And I want you to be a Christian."

"So do I, Father dear," answered Mary simply, the tears rushing into her eyes. "I want to be a Christian too."

"Yes, my love," he went on. "It is not that I do not think you a Christian. I do think you one. It is that I want you to be a downright real Christian, not one that is only trying to feel as a Christian ought to feel. I have lost so much precious time in that way!"

"Tell me," said Mary, clapping her other hand over his. "What would you have me do?"

"I will tell you," he replied. "At least I will try. A Christian is one that does what the Lord Jesus tells him. Neither more nor less than that makes a Christian. It is not even understanding the Lord Jesus that makes one a Christian. It is doing what he tells us that makes us Christians, and that is the only way to understand him. Peter says that the Holy Spirit is given to them that obey him: what else can that be but just actually, really doing what he says—just as if I were to tell you to go and fetch me my Bible, and you would get up and go. Did you ever do anything, my child, just because Jesus told you to do it?"

Mary did not answer immediately. She thought for a moment, then spoke.

"Yes, Father," she said, "I think so. Two nights ago, George was very rude to me—I don't mean anything bad, but you know he can be very rough."

"I know it, my child. And you must not think I don't care, because I think it better not to interfere. I am with you all the time."

"Thank you, Father. I know it. Well, when I was going to bed, I was still angry with him, so it was no wonder I found that I could not pray. Then I remembered how Jesus said we must forgive or we should not be forgiven. So I forgave George in my heart, and then I found I could pray."

The father stretched out his arms and drew her to him, murmuring, "My child! My Christ's child!" After a little pause, he began to speak again.

"It is a sad thing to hear those who desire to believe themselves Christians, talking and talking about this question and that, the discussion of which makes only for strife and not for unity—not a thought among them of the one command of Christ to love one another. I fear some are hardly content with not hating those who differ from them."

"I try, Father—and I think I do love everybody who loves him."

"Well, that is much—though it is not enough, my child. We must be like Jesus, and you know that it was while we were yet sinners that Christ died for us. Therefore, we must love all men, whether they are Christian or not."

"Tell me, then, what you want me to do, Father dear. I will do whatever you tell me."

"I want you to be just like the Lord Jesus, Mary. I want you to look out for his will, and find it, and do it. I want you not only to do it, though that is the main thing, when you think of it, but to look for it, to actively

seek it that you may do it. This is not a thing to be talked about much. You may think me very silent; but I do not always talk even when I am inclined to, for the fear that I might let my feelings out through talk, instead of doing something he wants of me with it. And how repulsive are those generally who talk the most. Our strength ought to go into conduct, not into talk—least of all into talk about what they call the doctrines of the gospel. The man who does what God tells him, sits at his Father's feet, and looks up in his Father's face. Such a man is a true Christian. And men had better be careful in how they criticize such a one, for he cannot greatly mistake his Father, and certainly will not displease him, when he is thus walking in obedience. Look for the lovely will of God, my child, that you may be its servant, its priest, its sister, its queen, its slave—as Paul calls himself. How that man did glory in his Master!"

A Daughter's Devotion, pp. 80–81

*But as he which hath called you is holy, so
be ye holy in all manner of conversation;
because it is written, Be ye holy;
for I am holy.*
1 Peter 1:15–16